Please Return

Solving Problems in Marriage

Solving Problems in Marriage

Guidelines for Christian Couples

by

Robert K. Bower

William B. Eerdmans Publishing Company
Grand Rapids, Michigan

Copyright © 1972 by William B. Eerdmans Publishing Company
All rights reserved
Library of Congress Catalog Card Number: 73-78020
ISBN 0-8028-1338-0
Printed in the United States of America

Contents

Preface

The alarming rate of marriage breakup in our society (in some areas as high as one divorce in every two marriages) calls for the use of every diagnostic and therapeutic tool available. One of the most common methods in treating personality and marital disorders is "bibliotherapy" — the use of books and other forms of professional literature. As every counselor and therapist knows, husbands and wives who are experiencing marital difficulty must in the final analysis carry a large part of the responsibility for devising a solution to their problem. No professional therapist or counselor can do it all. If couples will read about the nature, stresses, conflicts, and basic dynamics of marriage, they can begin to gain greater insight into their own situation and thereby contribute to the solution of the problems confronting them.

The appearance of an increasing number of written works on methods for solving marriage problems reinforces my conviction that reading material can be of invaluable assistance to a couple who find difficulties in their marriage relationship. Underlying any book about solving marital problems is the assumption that people and their circumstances are enough alike so principles found successful for treating one set of persons may well be applicable to others in similar situations.

The reader seeking help from this volume may find it profitable to open it at any chapter and read it without reference to the balance of the book, but he* may find it more helpful to read the volume straight through first and then refer to individual chapters for future guidance and direction. He may also find it helpful during periods of marital tension and conflict to reflect on the summary principles listed at the end of each chapter as a quick review.

The logic of the chapter arrangement points up the great importance of openness and self-disclosure (Chapter 1) as preliminary to any program of marital problem-solving. Openness between mates is stressed as essential to the practice of spouse acceptance (Chapter 2), the creation of healthy self-images (Chapter 3), and the implementation of methods for improving communication between husbands and wives (Chapter 4). Along with the need for openness there is a necessity for a New Testament, *agape* love to be present for the solution of marital conflicts. The dual note of openness and love is found throughout the book but comes out perhaps most strongly in the chapters on the problems of authority (Chapter 5), dividing responsibilities in the home (Chapter 6), achieving a personal identity for husbands and wives (Chapter 7), and attaining sexual compatibility and happiness (Chapter 8).

In order for Christian couples and those in the field of marriage, pastoral, or psychological counseling to profit most from the chapters in this volume, case history material has been provided — material from my own experience in conducting marriage counseling and therapy. All identifying data in the histories have, of course, been removed so that complete anonymity is assured.

* * *

I owe a debt of gratitude to all who have had a part in this undertaking. To the many clients who have shared

*In order to avoid the repetition of "he" and "she" and "his" and "her," the pronouns "he," "him," and "his" have been used throughout the book to refer to either gender.

their problems and difficulties with me in therapy sessions over the years, I am grateful. To Charmian Pugh who has given such excellent secretarial assistance and help, I offer my heartfelt thanks. Lastly, special thanks go to my wife Jean, who has given unstintingly of her time and effort and who constantly encouraged me throughout the period involved in the writing of the manuscript.

—Robert K. Bower

Pasadena, California

1. The Need for Openness in Marriage

Self-Disclosure

There are few experiences in life so deeply satisfying as the complete trust and openness that characterize the relationship of newly married couples. In the first months after the marriage ceremony, their attitude is likely to be: "We will never keep anything from one another as long as we live. Love can conquer all things; and if we have any problems, we will go to one another and talk them out, frankly, openly, and freely."

As time goes on, they both find reasons, many of them insignificant, for keeping certain matters concealed. The Christmas gift or birthday present that has been kept a secret and is designed to bring happiness may be the start. Later, it is a fact that is kept hidden because, if it were revealed, it might bring unhappiness or sorrow at a particular moment. Before many years pass, other reasons for withholding information arise, some of which appear to be for everyone's good and some of which may be selfish. After five or ten years of marriage, most couples have established an unfortunate pattern of limited openness. Both husband and wife have many secrets. The result is frequently a lack of integrity and honesty, patterns of manipulation, threatening statements, guilt feelings, and moderate to deep distrust.

Karl Barth speaks of the need for husbands and wives to be open with each other throughout life. Marriage motivated by love, he states,

> ... means experiencing ... the succession of unforeseeably many days of twenty-four hours and unforeseeably many years of fifty-two weeks, with the intimacy of an everyday and everynight companionship which *discloses everything on both sides.*[1]

Self-disclosure, which is the essence of honesty and integrity, is also seen by Sidney Jourard as vital to a sound marriage relationship and to an individual's mental health. He says that in relationships that are the most compatible with health, "each partner can communicate effectively and can *fully disclose himself* to the other."[2]

Needless Guilt Feelings

Couples tend to create problems for themselves when they are not open with one another about their innermost feelings. For example, guilt feelings may develop if a spouse makes a threat and then fails to follow through because he did not intend to carry it out from the very first. Since most threats are made when emotions are extremely intense, they are often irrational, unrealistic, and not seriously meant. The outcome, however, may be a sense of guilt.

Marge said to her husband, "If you go out with the fellows from work once more on our night out, I'm leaving you. I have had all I can take. I can't tolerate this any longer." Her husband's reply was a bristling one: "Oh, so that's the way you feel about me, is it? Well, you just watch me. No woman is going to tell me *what to do!"*

Marge's attack challenged her husband and his sense of independence. She was dictating what he could or could not do. Perhaps he had already decided to discontinue spending Friday nights with his friends, but now there is a

[1] *Church Dogmatics*, III/4, 187 (italics added).
[2] *Personal Adjustment*, p. 358 (italics added).

threat, a challenge to his right of individual determination. It could well be that Marge really did plan to leave her husband if he continued to neglect her on Friday nights, but if she was not serious about her threat and was hiding her intentions, there is a good chance that she will develop deep guilt feelings over her insincerity.

How could Marge have been open and honest about her real, intense feelings without making any threat or derogatory remarks about her husband and his activities? She might have said, "On Friday nights when I expect to go out with you but find myself sitting at home alone, it makes me furious." Had she chosen this approach, she would have informed her husband very honestly about her strong feelings, while avoiding the threat of directing his life by telling him what he must do. The husband would then have been free to decide whether or not he wished to spend Friday evenings with his wife, without appearing to lose his independence by being forced to yield to his wife's threats. The advantage of this approach is that it provides the spouse with freedom to act out of conscience and love rather than compulsion. And it is on this basis that couples should seek to build their marriages and solve their problems.

Marriage partners may also create guilt feelings for themselves by trying to bargain with one another as a means of solving problems, but in the process being more open than the situation warrants. This sort of inept or unwise self-disclosure may allow a mate to take advantage of his spouse. For example, a wife may say to her husband, "If you stop your drinking, I'll pay more attention to you. But right now your excessive drinking shows that you have no respect for me or for the children." By this "deal," the wife is creating a situation detrimental to both her welfare and his. He may stop drinking for a short period of time, but later resume his habit and demand more for stopping the next time. With each successive demand and each failure to stop his drinking, she adds to her guilt feelings by being completely open and discussing what it is that she hopes will "buy" him away from his problem, but always wondering whether she is offering enough. In doing this, she carries the major responsibility for his drinking since she assumes the task of offering him *enough* incentive to discontinue. A neurotic arrangement of this kind is likely to produce strong guilt feelings. Similar situations may involve a spouse's compulsive spending, gambling, excessive miserliness, or some equally aggravating behavior. In each case, once bargaining has begun a cycle starts and there is no easy end to the increasing demands placed on the partner attempting to improve the marriage.

One very effective method for handling such problems is to be very honest and open about the relationship and state only once — clearly and forcefully enough so it will be remembered — that good or appropriate behavior will be rewarded *nonverbally* and that all other behavior will be treated neutrally, with no criticism or negative remarks forthcoming. The reward itself must be genuine and well enough understood by both parties so that the acceptable behavior can be reinforced *without any statement that "this is for that."*

One reason for avoiding further statements about rewards is the resistance of many people to gifts or special attention if the underlying rationale is put into words. With this understanding a husband may stop his drinking (or other inappropriate behavior) and accept the increased attention from his wife. The outcome of the reward-reinforcement process is that a new habit is developed, based in part on love and appreciation. If he returns to his former behavior pattern, he cannot ask for increased attention as a requirement for discontinuing his practice since no such agreement was put into words after the initial understanding, and no bargaining spiral of greater and greater demands was ever begun. No further words are spoken about the nature of the problem. No criticisms or negative statements about the behavior problem are made. But each time the husband discontinues his inappropriate behavior the reward is given. In this way, the wife avoids a bargaining arrangement that would ultimately leave her without any resources with which to help him solve his problem.

Peace at Any Price

When difficulties arise at home, couples will often take the position that it is better to keep feelings down — to avoid conflict and rocking the boat — than to upset the tranquillity that exists. A policy of "Peace at Any Price," rather than of truth and integrity, is the way of life. In order to continue a peaceful atmosphere at home, white lies and other so-called nondamaging deceptions for maintaining the *status quo* are employed. A lack of integrity and feelings of guilt result from this philosophy, despite rationalizations about how white lies and other peace-promoting devices are justified by the ends obtained.

A wife asked her husband one night if he had ever had an affair prior to their marriage — a subject he had managed to avoid all through their courtship. During his time in the armed forces he had, in fact, spent some time with a woman who lived with him as his mistress. As a result of this affair, he was far more experienced in sexual techniques than was his wife. Also, his wife was not nearly as sexually satisfying to him as was the other woman. Yet he loved his wife and did not wish to hurt her, or cause her to feel inadequate. He, therefore, gave her a negative reply. According to him, he seemed to sense that a sexual panic might grip her if she had become aware of her deficiencies as a sexual partner.

Now it is generally true that spouses or couples who develop doubts about their sexual adequacy create emo-

15

tional blocks for themselves through their anxiety feelings. A self-defeating pattern arises: the more they think about trying to become adequate, the more anxious and inadequate they become. The husband in our illustration appeared to do the loving thing. Reuel Howe, however, advocates a different approach:

> It would be much better to have a disturbance over a real revelation of ourselves to another than it would be to have a false kind of peace in which the sense of belonging to each other becomes impossible. Mutual revelation is the answer to deception.[3]

Though the truth in the long run would perhaps have been advisable, the husband decided to evade the issue. He felt guilty about the deception, but justified it on the ground that he was sparing his wife some psychological pain and simultaneously avoiding emotional conflict with her. What he had done, of course, was to underestimate both the power of love to forgive and to overcome feelings of hurt and the possible damage to their relationship if the deception should be discovered at a later date.

One wife stated that her husband had kept something from her for a period of six years. Up to this time, she felt she knew his every thought. Suddenly she realized this was not the case, and it frightened her.

"If he has kept this secret from me for so long," she said to the therapist, "he might keep other thoughts from me. For instance, he might think of leaving me for a younger woman and never say anything about what might be wrong with our relationship." Since she was passing through the menopause, her fear was not unusual. Yet the husband gave no evidence of such thinking but, rather, was very much in love with his wife, who was attractive and sexually satisfying to him.

[3]*The Creative Years*, p. 118.

The very point in life at which she needed reassurance and a sense of trust and confidence in her husband was the time when she discovered his secretiveness, causing her to suspect possible deception in all of the relationships in the marriage.

Hobart Mowrer, dealing with the subject of honesty in personal relationships, states:

> We must once again recognize radical openness with the significant "others" in one's life, not only as the most effective means of "treatment," but also as the best form of *prevention,* as a *way of life.* Instead of being told that, as long as we are "normal" or "well," confession to our fellowmen is not necessary, we . . . should be led to see the virtue of . . . openness in general.[4]

As a guiding principle, when a spouse asks a question, it is probable that he possesses sufficient ego strength and has mobilized enough emotional resources to withstand the emotional impact of any answer whatever. The person who cannot handle the impact of an answer to such a question because it would be shattering to his personality will usually repress and refuse to ask it.

Should there be complete openness between spouses at all times? What if questions of a confidential nature are asked? Are some moments better than others for releasing information? Are there ways of wording statements so that an attitude of openness shows love and consideration and not rudeness, sarcasm, or discourtesy?

The answers to these questions depend upon many factors. There seems to be agreement on the importance of complete openness as the ideal or final goal. But how to achieve the goal without destroying a marriage requires great sensitivity and wisdom. Jourard cautions, and rightly so, against reckless and insensitive openness and self-disclosure:

[4]*The New Group Therapy,* p. 90.

It should not be construed from all the preceding discussion that the sheer *amount* of self-disclosure that goes on between participants in a relationship is an index of the health of the relationship or of the persons. *There are such factors as timing, interest of the other person, appropriateness, and effect of disclosures on either participant which must be considered in any judgment* . . . too much disclosure and too little disclosure may be associated with unhealthy personality, while some intermediate amount, under appropriate conditions and settings, is indicative of healthier personality.[5]

Couples must learn to know themselves well enough, then, to assess each other's emotional resources at any particular time. Physical illness, undue stress and tension, or a history of continual anxiety will dictate caution, so that negative or depressing statements will be made only when there is adequate emotional strength for handling them. After a number of years of married life, perceptive husbands and wives are usually able to assess or determine how much emotional material a partner can take without its causing an emotional upheaval.

David Mace points out that there may be rare situations in which complete openness is impractical:

It is by no means true that all married people, or even most of them, practice this unreserved mutual openness of heart toward one another. Yet it is likely that, *with the rare exceptions of matters that cannot be confided for some very good reason,* the degree to which husbands and wives share their thoughts and feelings represents the degree of depth and quality that they are able to achieve in their mutual fellowship.[6]

Should a spouse request information before conditions are appropriate for its disclosure, it may still be best to *begin* providing the answer by both a statement and a

[5]*Personal Adjustment*, pp. 353f. (italics added).
[6]*Whom God Hath Joined*, p. 59 (italics added).

question. In other words, to answer the question, "Is there anything you are withholding from me?", one might candidly say, "Yes, there is. But could we postpone discussing it for now?" The spouse is thus open enough to tell his mate that there *is* something he is keeping back. It may well be that the marriage relationship will not be materially influenced by this bit of undisclosed information. If it does become a serious problem, they might seek professional advice and counsel on how to handle it. In any case, if both spouses are aware that there could be something being withheld, then there has been no lie or deception. Though the degree of openness is not ideal, it is very likely the best arrangement under the circumstances. And the day may well come when the confidential information can be communicated with a minimum of disturbance to the marriage.

Expressions of Anger

If there is to be integrity in marriage, both partners must be open and upright, refusing to manipulate or take advantage of the other for selfish ends. This should encourage rather than hinder the expression of normal emotions, including anger, by marital partners. The spouse who exploits his mate's love and sympathy by being angry under the guise of "openness" and uses this to achieve his own goals is carrying on a manipulative process that could severely damage the marital relationship. On the other hand, if he has been wronged by an extremely negligent and emotionally (or physically) cruel mate, he has a right to be open and to express his anger (thereby releasing any potentially unhealthy feelings), thus informing his mate that he, too, is a person who is due proper respect.

George Bach, in his book on marital fighting, advocates expressions of anger as a means of showing love and concern, and thereby *improving* a marriage relationship rather than destroying it. This therapeutic method, he states, makes use of "aggression in the service of love."[7]

If anger is to be expressed as part of a desire to be open, it must be justifiable and appropriate. There are legitimate and illegitimate times to be angry, and there are right and wrong ways to express it. All *physical* expressions of anger should be banned. Throwing objects, striking, spanking, destruction of furniture—all such behavior can never solve problems in any lasting way.

To employ violence as a medium of communication may result in permanent physical or emotional damage. "I was able to take it until he struck me," or "I know now I'll *never* go back," a wife will say. Another wife may state, "The way he is now is fine, but it's too late. When he slapped me in the face and cut my lip that finished it for me." Obviously, the guilt feelings that develop over physical mistreatment of a spouse can be enormous. Integrity may rightfully call for an expression of emotion, but this should be justifiable in nature and appropriate, that is, nonviolent and preferably impersonal.

It is best to avoid attacking the personal traits or habits of a spouse, since this lowers his self-esteem, puts him on the defensive, and probably makes him unwilling to consider any behavior change.

Wrong (Wife in exasperation attacks husband with sarcasm): "You never seem to do anything right. How dumb can you get. Even a two-year-old could fix that faucet!" (The wife has attacked the intelligence and skill of the husband, thereby lowering his self-esteem.)

Right (Wife with exasperation): "Seeing that dripping faucet there really upsets me. It's been going on like that for a month!"

In the latter case, the wife refrained from attacking her husband's personality and yet informed him of her frustra-

[7] *The Intimate Enemy* (with P. Wyden), p. 352.

tion and disgust. Confronted by this approach, he will be less defensive, for there is no need to protect himself from attack. So he will feel *more* at liberty to fix the faucet according to his work schedule without developing a negative attitude toward his wife.

Some individuals find it difficult to express their emotions in words and resort to physical attacks in order to communicate a message to their mates. To solve this kind of problem, psychotherapists often employ semantic educational methods, providing such persons not only with the exact words and phrases to use in expressing their emotions properly but also opportunities to develop new modes of behavior through the use of guided discussion, role playing, and psychodrama.

Written Contracts

Although many counselors and therapists view with disfavor any kind of contract for the settlement of problems, others have found this technique helpful in many situations. The Conciliation Court of Los Angeles County has found a written contract to be of great assistance for identifying the problems and individual needs of couples contemplating divorce action. Each area of disagreement is explored with complete openness and honesty, and each area of life and its attendant responsibilities are covered in the sessions with the court counselor. Sex life, financial planning, occupational and educational plans, child care, religious training—all are discussed in detail and then inserted in the marriage contract. The contract numbers five pages in length and outlines the general responsibilities of each spouse in meeting the needs of his mate and family.

Lederer and Jackson suggest the same kind of openness in the assignment of responsibilities in the home:

> First Miriam and Ken are to sit down together and compile a list of the various duties performed and roles filled when they

are home together over a weekend. Such activities as cooking, cleaning, entertainment, and helping the kids with schoolwork will be listed. . . .

For the sake of experience and practice they should plan for the next several weekends to divide functions and tasks rigorously, agreeing in advance about which spouse is to take charge of each particular duty. . . . The procedure described here sounds very simple and mechanized, but in carrying it out, most couples will find to their surprise that although they have been assuming that each has his assigned tasks, actually . . . tasks have not been clearly assigned, and . . . status struggles occur when husband and wife attempt to take over a task at the same time, or when one interferes with the other's performance.[8]

A written contract (or agreement) may be a satisfactory arrangement for a short period of time, but ultimately love, rather than a contract, should become the uniting force in a couple's life. Otherwise, they tend to be overly demanding of each other, as though their marriage were nothing more than a business arrangement, requiring that certain conditions be met in order to fulfil the terms of the contract.

Ideally, marriage should be a covenant, characterized by love and trust and a willingness to be transparent and open with one's mate. Without this, it becomes empty and meaningless and devoid of real satisfaction. The road back for couples who have all but given up on their marriage may profitably include a written contract, but this must lead eventually to trust and love in order for the marriage to survive and be purposeful for both partners.

Necessity of Risk

There is little question that husbands and wives who determine within themselves to be open, honest, and un-

[8]*The Mirages of Marriage*, p. 264.

selfish in their relationships are running a great risk. A spouse who demonstrates his integrity in all relations with his mate may experience rejection in the form of sarcasm and doubt. There may be remarks like, "Don't tell me you are going to try *again* to make changes in your personality. You have been trying for years, and it just doesn't work." Or, a spouse will admit that he has been wrong, and then discover that instead of gaining understanding and help from his mate, the information he has confided is being used to win friends and family members to the other's side. Or, he may disclose a desperate need, hoping that it will elicit sympathy from the spouse, only to discover that the knowledge is used to manipulate him for the other's selfish ends.

The emotional depression—and sometimes despair—that can result from interpersonal risks may lead one to say, "Never again will I open myself up like that. It hurt too much." Yet if it is true that a husband and wife are a unity, in some unique way, then they should aim at complete openness and knowledge of each other, instead of being a split, unintegrated marital unit. In the case of individuals, an ego that is fragmented and disorganized is not healthy. This is true of what might be called the marital ego of a husband and wife as well. As a single entity, they should avoid a split marital ego with its hidden information, hidden needs, and unshared disappointments. How can a wife be a helpmate to her husband if she is not informed of matters that require her assistance? How can a husband love his wife if she withholds information from him about her needs and desires? Husbands and wives should endeavor to become one, to become open with one another, in their thinking, feeling, and actions as much as is humanly possible.

Though the risks involved in being open are often great, the rewards are even greater. One caution should be noted. Attitudes and behavior patterns change slowly, sometimes taking months or even years. The spouse who begins to practice personal integrity and openness after years of manipulation and secretiveness should not expect immediate changes in himself or in his mate. Perhaps sudden, even miraculous changes will take place, but this is the exception, not the rule. Lederer and Jackson state that the period required for behavior change may be a long one, even with professional help.

> If a couple has serious marital problems, they are likely to see their therapist for one or two years. This doesn't mean that they will necessarily see him once a week during the entire period. If they make considerable progress in six months or a year, less frequent sessions may be sufficient thereafter. On the other hand, new and different problems may suddenly occur which require brief periods of more intensive therapy. Even when the process of working out a marital problem involves two steps forward and one step back, the net accomplishment may be considerable.[9]

In the final analysis, a person must be true to himself. A major part of the identity of a married man or woman involves those factors of sexuality that influence the way he or she relates to his spouse. And as a man, or a woman, there is the deep desire to be open and to be one with the opposite sex, physically, emotionally, mentally, spiritually, and in all other dimensions of personality. Man as man and woman as woman have implanted within them the deep drive and desire to be one. Obviously, many forces oppose this drive and sometimes defeat it, but the innate desire is there, nevertheless, implanted in man by his Creator.

Summary

1. Every effort should be made to establish sincerity and honesty between a husband and wife.
2. It is best to avoid the use of threats as a means of manipulating a spouse. It tends to deprive him of his

[9]*Ibid.*, p. 447.

sense of independence and frequently leads to guilt feelings in the person making the threats.

3. The marital motto "Peace at Any Price" may involve "white lies" in order to maintain tranquillity, but it tends eventually to create increasing falsehood and hypocrisy. It is better to be open about a matter (assuming that circumstances are appropriate), or to make no comment at all, rather than to permit oneself to develop habits of deception, however well-meaning they may be.

4. If honesty has been absent in a relationship for a considerable time, a sudden decision to be "open" with a spouse who may be undergoing severe physical illness or undue stress may be more than he can emotionally handle. A person must assess the spouse's emotional strength to receive the material to be disclosed and select an appropriate time for disclosure. The goal should be openness, but how and when that goal should be reached must be cautiously and carefully ascertained.

5. Integrity also implies the right to express anger if one truly feels it. Anger, however, should be appropriately expressed, using words but not violent actions to express the emotion.

6. Self-giving love should bind a couple together. A written contract may serve to move toward this end if used judiciously and not legalistically or rigidly.

7. After all factors have been considered by a couple, a degree of risk is necessary in deciding to try and make a marriage work. This is true at the time marriage is begun and is true for most of its critical periods. The risk, however, must be accepted by both parties if problems are to be solved satisfactorily.

2. Learning Acceptance

Whenever two or more persons live or work in close proximity, there will be discussions and problems, occasionally sharp disagreements. This is as true for married couples as for anyone else. How they perceive their problems and how they conduct their discussions—whether there is a willingness to accept one another with some imperfections, or a too-idealistic, perfectionistic attitude between them—are highly significant factors in determining their future welfare and happiness.

Danger of Idealistic Thinking

Every couple entering marriage has an ideal or a feeling of what marriage should be like and how happiness can best be achieved. In the mental picture that each paints for himself of a marriage characterized by "true love," no one makes any serious mistakes, and there are seldom any tensions or unresolved problems. The ingredients that go into this picture are derived from many sources—parental example, magazine stories and articles, television programs or motion pictures, and others. Unfortunately, most people extract the "good" or positive features from these sources in making up their mental picture of marriage and ignore the negative elements almost entirely. As a result, idealistic or perfectionistic images of what "our marriage ought to be like" develop. But there are limits on the extent to which a spouse can adapt in trying to attain the ideal of a perfect marriage by attempting to be the perfect mate.

> There are limits to how much a person can change his personality structure in order to meet the needs of a partner; and often the changes which would be required to keep a marriage going would be personality changes in a direction away from health. Thus, one partner may need the other to be an absolute paragon of perfection. . . . No amount of feasible change could make the partner attain those ideals. Further, no amount of personality therapy is successful in altering the needs of the spouse who demands perfection.[1]

A realistic view of both marriage and personality, therefore, calls for two essential attitudes to exist in any successful marriage venture: (1) a desire to build and improve the marital relationship, and (2) a willingness at the same time to accept imperfections in a spouse as part of a realistic philosophy of life, recognizing that all humans have their limitations and weaknesses.

One young couple who came for therapy had a definite need for accepting each other's personalities and yet moving toward a more realistic attitude about their future.

Jim and Mary had been husband and wife for several years. He was interested in completing his education and gaining some experience in his particular line of work. She was willing to continue at her job, she said, in order for him to achieve his goals. She told him, however, that she was interested in beginning a family as soon as possible.

In time, it became obvious that he was not particularly concerned about a family and was continuing to put more and more emphasis upon his vocation. When they originally discussed their marriage plans, Jim and Mary had taken it for granted that each would work with the other in fulfilling his dream. (After all, this was the way television often seemed to portray marriage, with both partners

[1] Sidney Jourard, *Personal Adjustment*, p. 391.

finding fulfilment for all personal needs.) This was the ideal that each held: she would help him achieve his goals and he would help her achieve hers. But her picture included children within the first five years of marriage, whereas his included children with no time factor stipulated. The ideal wife to him was one who was willing to forgo a family until he had completed his education and achieved relative success in his chosen career, however long that might be. Her picture of the ideal husband was one who would understand her desire to have a family as early as possible—and certainly not wait more than five years to begin one.

Once Jim and Mary became aware that their thinking and needs were idealistic, they were able to come to an understanding of what was realistic for them. She agreed to help him complete a specified part of his rather ambitious program, and he consented to plan with her a family by a mutually determined date.

Other persons may hold as an ideal goal a dominant emotional image of the thrill, the warmth, and the seemingly never-ending bliss of the romantic days of courtship. Such an experience is seldom, if ever, forgotten. Many wives, and occasionally husbands, do not recognize this as a stage in life, and insist on making it a continuous experience, year in and year out. This is an idealistic goal, almost impossible to achieve.

Family Influences

Psychologists, counselors, and others who work with disturbed marriages are familiar with the fact that early family influences are highly significant in determining an individual's marital behavior.

> The behavior in the adult is a continuation of responses learned in childhood. Therefore, if we wish to speak of the meaning of disturbed marital relationships, we must shift from

an exclusive focus on the adult behavior to consideration of the infantile level, and obtain a comprehensive view of the patient's total life experience of persons and things.[2]

What may appear to be completely irrational on the surface, therefore, may be perfectly logical within the framework of a spouse's background, and, for that reason, acceptable in part. Consequently, it is expedient to gain a knowledge and understanding of a mate's home and early childhood relationships and experiences.

Bob and Joan argued constantly over the organization of their home, especially the time for meals and the type of food to be served. Bob was a "meat and potato man" and arrived home at various times for the evening meal, frequently 30 to 45 minutes late. Over a period of several years, Joan's frustration created gradually increasing feelings of hostility toward Bob for his lack of interest in balanced diets and promptness until one night Bob found her almost hysterical over the situation. Eventually, he came to recognize (and to accept) what was behind his wife's condition.

Joan's brother was a diabetic. His physician had given orders that he should eat his meals at exactly the same time each day, and that he should be provided with a specific type of balanced diet. The entire family had adjusted their schedules to meet that program. If meals were delayed just a few minutes, tension and sometimes anger would develop, usually on the part of the mother or father, creating a very anxiety-ridden atmosphere in the home.

Over the years, a mental and emotional pattern had become an integral part of Joan's personality: meals must be on time and well-balanced, or tension and hostility would result. These patterns of thinking continued, largely

[2]E. H. Mudd and A. Krich (eds.), *Man and Wife*, p. 41.

at the unconscious level, into her married life. Once Bob understood this, he began to arrive home much more promptly, though not always at the exact time; and she in turn learned to accept some lateness from him with a degree of equanimity, especially if he telephoned her about the nature and length of his delay.

Berelson and Steiner, in their review of the research on human behavior, found that opinions, attitudes, and beliefs "are 'inherited' from one's parents: people learn them early in life and the learning persists into adulthood."[3] This was the case for Ron and Gladys.

Ron grew up in a community that was relatively poor. His father was a laborer with a rather low income. Advanced education, life insurance, long-range planning of vacations, savings accounts, and the like were outside the area of living for the family as a result of their limited finances and day-to-day living. Ron's wife Gladys, however, came from a middle-class home in which education, insurance, and savings were part of their way of life.

When Ron and Gladys married, their love for each other was strong and loyal, and both were extremely happy. When the first child arrived, Gladys suggested the possibility of life insurance as a protection for her and especially the child. Ron disagreed, "My folks didn't carry any life insurance on themselves and neither will we." As the child grew older and reached the teen-age years, the wife suggested a savings account so he could attend college upon graduation from high school. "My folks didn't send me to college," the husband snapped. "If he wants to go, let him earn his own way. I've gotten along all right without a college education, so can he."

To this, the wife tried to reply in a tactful way, "But things are so different today. College training is necessary

[3]*Human Behavior*, p. 562.

for obtaining a great many jobs, and the cost of college is rising so fast that it's more difficult for a young person to pay his entire way."

The husband answered, "Well, as far as I'm concerned, a college education is a luxury, not a necessity, and so I'm not going to put money aside for that."

Ron's attitude led Gladys to feel that he did not love their child and that he was unrealistic. Moreover, his refusal to do any kind of long-range planning—whether for their son's education, insurance, summer vacations, or retirement—tended increasingly to irritate her. In time, she came to recognize the family influences that had shaped Ron's thinking. And though Ron would seldom admit it in the therapy sessions, it was evident that he began to gain some insight into his own personality dynamics. Eventually, his wife took the position of accepting him as he was (and as she had married him), with the result that he made an independent decision to open a savings account for their child, and later began to discuss their retirement program with her.

Family influences are also evident in the attitudes one holds toward love, sexual intercourse, and sexual relationships in general.

Art and Jane were fairly well matched in terms of social class, religion, and education. But sexually, they found themselves far apart. He was not overly demanding, but he did expect to have sexual relations as frequently as the typical husband of his age. His wife, brought up in a family in which the mother was totally negative about sexual matters, had an entirely different attitude. Sex was something to be "endured" by a woman and then only when absolutely necessary. Although physically attractive to her husband, she grew tense and antagonistic toward him if he desired to love and caress her in any way.

31

As a consequence, he became irritable and at times extremely angry. This caused her, in return, to become angry with him because he was not loving or understanding— understanding of the fact that she was doing her best to love and please him. Each caused the other to be angry in a spiraling fashion until the marriage was on the point of collapse.

In counseling and therapy, it was only after Art came to realize the negative effect that Jane's mother had had on her attitude toward sex that he began to appreciate how much effort his wife was actually exerting to please him. It was necessary for him to accept her just as she was, with all of her deficiencies. His doing this relieved her of any necessity to "prove herself," and with this acceptance came a sense of freedom and relaxation that helped her be more positive toward him (he no longer became angry if things were not completely satisfying). This, in turn, released some of the warm and affectionate feelings she had held toward him during courtship and honeymoon. This accepting attitude gradually helped remove her sexual inhibitions, and a normal pattern of sexual relations was established. If Art had not accepted Jane as she was, however, the most likely outcome would have been complete frustration and hostility for both, with serious thoughts of separation.

The Fallacy of Comparison

"Look at how much furniture our friends have in their apartment, and they were married the same time as we were. Not only that, they are driving a brand new Thunderbird!"

So spoke a young wife of two years who had just decided to leave her husband and take their child with her. It was true that their friends did enjoy a luxuriously furnished apartment and one of the latest model automobiles. But the friends were in debt over their heads. The husband and his complaining wife, on the other hand, owed nothing on their furnishings or their car. Besides, they were not renting, but purchasing a house and building up equity. The husband's job, though not too well paying, was one in which he was vitally interested and held great promise of advancement. When this was explained to the young complaining wife, she stopped comparing their status with the other couple's and began to accept her husband and their life together more realistically. The problem in this case had been both unwillingness to accept her husband's thrift plus a tendency to make faulty comparisons.

False comparisons can involve things other than financial status:

Henry Brown sarcastically asked his wife, "What are you so irritated about? Tim's wife entertains at least three times a week. I ask you to do so twice a week and you get emotionally upset. And you certainly get a lot more rest than his wife does. She's up at six every morning and you don't open your eyes until seven or eight. What's wrong?"

Unfortunately, Henry's wife agreed with him. If Tim's wife could get along on less sleep and still entertain three times a week, so could she. No one was going to outdo her! Within six months she experienced complete physical exhaustion and was committed to a hospital for psychiatric care.

The case history of this patient revealed that, since childhood, she had been highly nervous in social situations and had needed more rest than the average person of her age. Also, her mother had been extremely sensitive over the years, giving evidence of perfectionistic traits and withdrawal from general interpersonal activities. On the basis of these disclosures, the therapist hypothesized that Mrs.

Brown had inherited a nervous system highly sensitive to stress (further conditioned by the critical and perfectionistic attitudes of her mother). The Browns formulated a manageable program that took into consideration her heredity and family background. This was in harmony with what Hans Selye says:

> When a human being is born—unless he wants to kill himself— he cannot stop . . . before he has completed his mission on earth. Yet he too can do much, through voluntary choice of conduct, to get as far as possible *with a given bodily structure and supply of adaptation energy,* under given social conditions. For instance, he can live and express his personality at a tempo and in a manner best suited to his inherited talents, under the prevailing conditions.[4]

Henry, following the principles for relieving stress, cooperated with his wife by limiting the number of social engagements to what she could comfortably handle. He came to accept her need for more rest than other women and no longer complained about her extra sleep. His wife gained insight into her physical make-up and planned her activities more realistically. Both learned to accept her traits as they were and to adjust their lives accordingly.

When husbands and wives begin to recognize that we are all different,[5] damaging comparisons will cease and marriages will be happier. This does not mean to suggest that comparisons are always to be avoided. Without comparison, for example, it is difficult to discover how one is progressing at school or on the job. Without comparison of various makes and models, one cannot discover which automobile or refrigerator or radio best suits his needs. But when we compare personalities, and demand that they perform equally, we deny their individuality. We ignore genetic factors, the effects of traumatic childhood experiences that condition an individual (such as cruelty on the

[4]*The Stress of Life,* p. 279 (italics added).
[5]*Ibid.,* p. 301.

part of an alcoholic father, rejection by one's mother, or a terrifying sexual assault by a stranger), and the impact of difficult and frustrating adult experiences (for example, combat, loss of self-esteem through prolonged unemployment, or bereavement through fire or automobile accident). Such experiences tend to modify and influence the development and functioning of our personalities. To state that all persons, therefore, should conform to a single pattern of living is unscientific and clinically untenable.

Uniqueness of the Individual

The tendency to expect equal performance from all persons opposes the concept of the uniqueness of the individual with his own kind and intensity of needs. What satisfies one person may not satisfy another. Instead of accusing one another of a "lack of interest," or "lack of love," husbands and wives should endeavor to learn each other's needs and to what degree they can be met. Acceptance, of course, should pervade any discussion of needs because "a man can be helped only if he feels understood and accepted, as he is. . . . A generous acceptance is then for him a reflection of the mercy of God. For God loves us not for our virtues but for our need."[6]

A starting point for understanding a person involves asking what needs other persons of equivalent backgrounds have in an equivalent situation? This does not suggest that the spouse should be coerced toward such a standard or norm. It merely serves as a place to *begin* discussing personal needs. If a husband and wife find through open and honest discussion that they have special needs apart from the usual standard or norm, they should accept such needs and set out to build a mutually agreeable program for meeting them. Therapists have found that when spouses are willing to accept each other as they are and to

[6]Paul Tournier, *To Understand Each Other*, p. 49.

work together on their problems over a sufficient period of time, they can usually develop a style of life that brings meaning and happiness into their marriage.

Even in matters of religious faith acceptance is of great value, as Keith Miller attests. After numerous efforts to bring his wife to the point of conversion, he finally (and wisely) says:

> "Honey, I can't deny the tremendous things which have happened to me these past two years because of trying to give my future to the finding of God's will. But I have been wrong in trying to force all this on you. No one forced it on me. I'm sorry I tried (however unconsciously) to manipulate you by taking you to all these meetings, etc., to get you converted. I am really sorry." I went on to tell her, "when we got married I didn't sign up to *change* you, just to *love* you . . . and I do, just as you are."[7]

This is one of the marks of the mature person: that he "is able to accept things and people the way they are."[8]

Many people will deny that they have the necessary qualities and ego strength to accept their spouses as they are. In time, however, they usually discover greater resources within themselves than they suspected. There must be a recognition of the "differentness" of people, along with complete acceptance, honesty, and willingness for self-disclosure, if needs are to be met and the tensions of married life reduced and satisfaction achieved.

Misconceptions About the Nature of Marriage

Were it not for the prevalence of misunderstandings about the nature of marriage, psychological acceptance of spouses might not be so crucial a factor. But when marital misconceptions are combined with the impatience of husbands and wives over the normally slow process of person-

[7] *The Taste of New Wine*, p. 51.
[8] Reuel Howe, *The Creative Years*, p. 199.

ality change, it becomes imperative that mates learn to accept each other as they are. One must be content with his spouse as he is without asking for any *immediately* perceptible changes. This can diminish the tension that so often prevents the very changes of personality being sought.

One common misconception is that obviously needed improvements in personalities can be brought about quickly and easily. In reality, personality traits tend to be fairly stable, as Bloom has pointed out in *Stability and Change in Human Characteristics,* though they can change significantly in the early and middle adult years under appropriate circumstances.[9]

Another misconception held by many husbands and wives is that the adjustment in personality made by both spouses should eventually lead to a condition of absolutely no tension or anxiety in the marriage relationship. What they fail to realize is that wherever several persons are intimately engaged in the pursuit of common goals there will always be tension, conflict, and discussion about how best to achieve those goals. Can a sense of responsibility (a most important factor for achieving a successful marriage) ever exist without tension? An absence of tension produces bland, irresponsible, nonmotivated individuals who could not care less about self and family. In the light of this, a certain degree of anxiety should be expected in everyday, normal living. If this anxiety is not too great, it can have a definitely positive value.

A third misconception is that marriage should be a continual experience of ideal happiness and bliss. What most couples would like to preserve is the thrill they shared during courtship and the first months of marriage. But if they look closely, they will find that life is filled with both high and low moments of emotion. Studies have shown that individuals normally encounter both "peak

[9]See Benjamin Bloom's volume, *Stability and Change in Human Characteristics.*

experiences" and "valley experiences" in life, rather than experiencing one or the other type continually.[10] An expression commonly used to describe the period of peak-experiences in early marriage is that of "romantic love"; it is this type of love that many couples seek to maintain on a permanent basis. Data have shown that the ideal of continuous romantic love is relatively unrealistic. Lederer and Jackson, for example, state that:

> To maintain continuously a union based on love is not feasible for most people. Nor is it possible to live in a permanent state of romance. Normal people should not be frustrated or disappointed if they are not in a *constant* state of love.[11]

To be sure, there will be romantic "peak experiences" in the marriage, but there will also be the normal nonpeak experiences, and these are as much a part of authentic living.

A fourth misconception frequently heard in the beginning stage of marital counseling and therapy is that once romantic love is lost it cannot be recovered. "Our marriage is dead," said one woman, "the romance is completely gone out of our life." With this her husband agreed. Yet realistic and mature persons will continue to work at their marriage, drawing on the resources of a deep commitment to be faithful even when romantic love has all but disappeared.

Brunner says that marriage is "based not on love but on fidelity. Fidelity is the ethical element which enhances natural love, and only by its means does the natural become personal. It is, therefore, the only quality which can guarantee the permanence of the marriage relation." [12]

---

[10]For a discussion of peak experiences, see Abraham Maslow, *Religions, Values, and Peak-Experiences.* Although the concept of peak experience is directed largely toward the area of religion, it applies equally well to the value of love.

[11]*The Mirages of Marriage,* p. 59.

[12]*The Divine Inperative,* p. 357.

A psychologically mature spouse will recognize that no marriage is perfect, but if a couple is willing to identify and analyze their problems, solutions can usually be found. Romantic love or romantic "peak experiences" can be recovered and enjoyed once again, though they do require time and effort.

A final misconception we should discuss is the belief that if romance is present in a marriage a couple will be supremely happy. More than one married couple has found this to be insufficient. "Oh yes, the romantic aspect of our life is perfect," a couple may say, "but *where* are we going? What is our *purpose* in life? What is our *identity* as a married couple?" Increasingly, husbands and wives are finding their partners to be inadequate if "romantic love" alone is what holds them together. This is not to minimize the romantic dimension of marriage, for it is highly important. But more is sought. The husband seeks success in his work. The wife becomes interested in greater security for the family, especially the children. And other important objectives in life appear: establishing an identity in a depersonalizing culture, fulfilling one's God-given abilities, becoming a whole and complete person.

Apparently, as one moves through life, his goals are constantly changing. Early in life, romantic love is a coveted physical and emotional goal. Without the satisfaction that comes from the experience of romance, marriage loses much of its significance and purpose. But during the middle years of married adult life, the need for a sense of success at one's vocation and forming an identity become of prime importance, with the romantic objective playing an equal or lesser part. In the later years of marriage, as energy levels and drive for sexual satisfaction slowly diminish, emphasis moves toward completing one's identity and consolidating or "rounding out" life's program. Security, satisfaction in "having run a good race," and a feeling that one has contributed to the best of his ability characterize this period, along with a hope that one can accomplish even more with the skills, experience, and wisdom gained over the years.

Of course, serious physical illness, surgery, automobile accidents, and similar factors tend to make it difficult for husbands and wives to coordinate their life objectives. Unless there is a recognition, therefore, of the need for acceptance—not only of one's spouse but of many of the events in life—and for communication about these, intolerably high levels of anxiety can result, as well as irritation, dissatisfaction, and deep disappointment for both.

With the acceptance of what existence as a human being involves, however, couples can face the problems of life, as difficult as they are, and set their goals or modify them as necessary. This calls for courage to be open and honest. It is an adventure in interpersonal relationships that will make them emotionally uncomfortable at times. But it is the only way if one is going to accept the responsibility of being a truly constructive human being. Normal marriage is a struggle, ridden with anxiety. And in order to achieve a sense of satisfaction and joy in it, acceptance must permeate all of one's life, whatever the circumstances and however difficult they may be.

Forgiveness

The road from acceptance to authentic forgiveness is a truly long one for most husbands and wives. Couples seem to have little difficulty in offering forgiveness on an intellectual level, but when it comes to the emotional level there may be reluctance and resistance born of bitter experience. A husband may say to his wife, "I'm sorry about what I did. Please forgive me." But if this request is purely on the intellectual plane, as it may well be, she will sense that his whole person is not involved, and she will be skeptical. The impact of the wrongdoing and the remorse connected with it may not be enough to assure her that he will not repeat it. If she should, however, feel a genuine change in her husband's entire personality—including the emotional level—so that by attitude, word, and action he manifests a true interest in changing his behavior, it will be easier for her to forgive him intellectually *and* emotionally.

Although forgiveness is seldom easy to grant, acceptance may be a first step towards it, for it implies hope and faith that the good once evident is still latent and can be recovered. The husband or wife who willingly accepts a mate must do so not only in word but in attitude, which means avoiding criticism on *both* the verbal and nonverbal levels. Biting words and critical attitudes (revealed by such signs as looks of disgust, turning the back in rejection, exasperated sighs, or looks of doubt and skepticism) must be checked, and if at all possible eliminated. Inner attitudes are as important as outward ones when seeking to show a genuinely accepting spirit.

Along with this accepting attitude the opportunity must come for renewing marital relationships without loss of self-respect on the part of the accepted mate. In very few marital problems does the fault lie completely with one mate. It is unrealistic and unfair for a mate, therefore, to hold that his partner is solely to blame. An accepting attitude permits the spouse to maintain his self-respect, and acknowledges that at some points he has probably made courageous attempts to improve the marriage, that he may have been greatly influenced by his family background, and that the accepting spouse is also human, and therefore imperfect. Acceptance stresses greater understanding and empathy—the forerunners of genuine forgiveness.

Repression versus Suppression

"I can forgive, but I can't forget. I try to forget. I promise that I will never bring the subject up again, and yet it persistently forces its way into my mind day after day. And whenever we have an argument, I just can't seem

41

to control my emotions. I drag in the past just to irritate my husband."

What this wife is doing is trying to repress the unpleasant thoughts connected with events for which she had forgiven her husband. Every time a painful subject enters her consciousness, she immediately tries to ignore it. Psychologically, she is making an effort to push her negative thoughts into the unconscious rather than deal with them realistically. Consequently, they remain submerged for a short time, only to reappear during a heated argument or discussion.

The fact of the matter is that few of us can forget traumatic and highly emotional experiences in which we have been wronged. They force their way into our consciousness against our will and, if we are not careful, create guilt feelings because we have not forgotten though we have forgiven. The best a human being can do is forgive and make a *sincere effort* to forget.

What can a person do if he is troubled by this kind of unpleasant memory? Instead of refusing to consider these memories, he should look at them clearly, identify the problem or stimulus that brought them back to his consciousness, recall any act of forgiveness, and then, without undue reflection on such thoughts and their corresponding incidents, assign them to the recesses of the mind. As Coleman indicates, suppression (as opposed to repression) " 'puts the idea out of mind' and thinks of other things; . . . it is deliberate, and the individual knows what he is doing."[13] He should refuse to reflect on the events at great length, for he knows he will elicit the strong negative feelings that originally accompanied the experience and thereby create anxiety for himself. He also runs the risk of dealing with the material once more, with all of the hostility that may have previously gone with it.

Suppression differs from repression in that it does not

[13]*Abnormal Psychology and Modern Life,* p. 92.

avoid identifying the feelings connected with thoughts arising in the mind, as repression does. Suppression evaluates thoughts when they come into consciousness and then puts them out if they are unhealthy. It can work closely with acceptance and forgiveness. Together, suppression, acceptance, and forgiveness mean realistically and appropriately considering the facts for what they are. Though suppression and acceptance are difficult to carry out, to forgive and forget is even more difficult, but when achieved is undoubtedly a reflection in man of the very nature of God Himself.

Summary

1. Discussions and disagreements are inevitable whenever two or more persons live or work together. Married persons are not immune to this fact of life. How they perceive their problems and seek to solve them is most important for their general happiness.
2. Each person entering into marriage brings with him a picture of how he would like the marriage to function. Since no two persons can agree on everything in detail, there will be differences in the pictures they have. Only the idealist thinks that his is right and the other's is wrong. Realistic thinking calls for both to make changes and adjustments in their marital behavior in a spirit of love and concern.
3. Acceptance of one's spouse becomes easier when his family background, behaviors, attitudes, and values are studied.
4. Mates should allow their spouses sufficient time— perhaps months, or a year or two—to make changes in thinking, feeling, and acting, since attitudes, habits, and behavior patterns tend to change gradually.
5. Each person is born with a unique pattern of traits. Some are more intelligent than others; some inherit more sensitive nervous systems than others; some can

take more physical stress than others. Although comparisons between persons may be fairly valid for many situations, for marriage partners to make comparisons with other couples is neither practical nor scientific. Such comparisons are frequently misleading and thus must be used with the greatest of caution.

6. Misconceptions about marriage include the following:

(A) Love will automatically help a mate change his personality suddenly.

Fact: Love undoubtedly motivates change, but personality changes usually occur gradually and require time and effort.

(B) No tension should exist in a marriage.

Fact: Wherever two persons try to work together there are always disagreements and tensions—unless one is completely passive with no will, no convictions, and no goals.

(C) Only "passionate," "romantic" love should be present in a mature marriage.

Fact: "Romantic" love is desirable, but it functions as a means of binding a husband and wife to each other as they begin their journey together *toward* mature love. There must be room for the love and nurturing of children and the pursuit of a vocation. There will be many romantic "peak experiences" within mature love, but a constant experience of "romance" is neither socially desirable nor reasonable in terms of the other dimensions of life which call for the attention, time, and energy of the individual.

(D) If a marriage has little or no love apparent in it, nothing can be done for it and it should be dissolved.

Fact: The spark of love can be rekindled, as clinical data in marital therapy reveal; moreover, marriages with some love can still be relatively stable.

7. Acceptance of a mate with his imperfections and improper actions does not necessarily imply forgiveness of these. Instead, it avoids both open and silent criticism of him and takes the position that, for the foreseeable future, no personality changes will be expected but every effort made to maintain a tolerable relationship. (Implicit, of course, is the hope that the situation will improve, but this hope does not guide the actions of the couple. They accept each other as they are.) Forgiveness may or may not appear subsequently.

8. Genuine forgiveness involves the whole person, including his intellectual and emotional being. A spouse may state on an intellectual plane that he forgives, but emotionally he may find it very difficult to do. It is better to forgive, of course, with one's whole personality than to offer forgiveness purely on an intellectual level. Honesty, in this, as in other cases, is crucial for both mates.

3. Creating Healthy Self-Images

Realistic Self-Concepts

As human beings, our interest in truth should lead us to seek realistic and accurate perceptions of ourselves. Only in this way can we make progress in personal growth and development.

If one's thinking is distorted to the extent of seeing himself as completely lacking in good qualities, the result will be unhealthy attitudes of low self-esteem and unworthiness. No one, of course, can be characterized as wholly bad or completely negative. Everyone has some positive traits that make him valuable to himself and to others. Yet if he does not recognize and accept these traits, he will possess a self-image that is negative.

There are also those who go to the other extreme, who hold a completely positive attitude, declaring that everyone is perfectly happy and satisfied.

George worked as a foreman in a manufacturing plant, but was hoping to set himself up in a small business within a few years. The image he held of himself was of a handsome, hard-working young man who was bound for success and idolized by a happy wife.

Both he and his wife Eleanor sacrificed and deprived themselves of the most inexpensive pleasures month after month. George, for the most part, saw himself "on top of the world." But his mental images were too optimistic. His wife was gradually losing interest, and though he thought she was happy, she had already become bored and disillusioned. Suddenly one day he realized that she was deeply in love with another man.

"I want to live, I want to enjoy life. I want to experience the wonderful, the beautiful, the joyous in life," she said. "I'm tired of a boring, uninteresting, depriving life."

Her husband was shocked. What he had heard was simply unbelievable to him. But it was true.

When George and Eleanor came for therapy, it was soon apparent that he had been living in an unreal world, insensitive to his wife's emotional needs. His own personality defects completely escaped him because of his overemphasis on his positive traits and repression of the negative ones. One of the therapeutic goals for George, therefore, was achieving a more realistic appraisal of himself.

A blind preoccupation with good traits and images, such as George's, can be as dangerous as an obsession with negative, pessimistic traits and images. The aim of every individual, however, should be to achieve an honest and accurate understanding of himself and all reality. As Jourard has said:

> The more accurate the individual's self-concept, and the more congruent one with the other are his self-ideal, self-concepts, public selves, and real self, then the less readily can a person be threatened. . . . The individual with a healthy self-structure can face and admit all of his motives and feelings and all of his past and present actions.[1]

This kind of knowledge will include recognition of both one's positive and negative qualities. Such an accurate and realistic view of the self should lead to a healthy and satisfying self-image—healthy, that is, in terms of recognizing those areas of life and personality that call for improvement and those that require acceptance.

[1] *Personal Adjustment*, p. 181.

The tension between the need to accept oneself—with both positive and negative traits—and the need to improve and grow is a matter of concern for everyone. The Bible expresses this tension when it states, on the one hand, that we are "to *grow* in grace" and to be conformed to the image of Christ (see II Pet. 3:18 and Rom. 8:29), implying personal improvement through continuous growth, but, on the other hand, that we are to be *content* with the state or condition in which we find ourselves (Phil. 4:11; see also Heb. 13:5). Insofar as this tension is not overwhelming, a healthy image of the self will emerge. One must remember that there is no growth without some tension,[2] but in order to avoid harmful tension one must learn to accept himself. If one becomes unduly obsessed with either the *status quo* or with personality improvement, unhealthy attitudes are usually the outcome.

Resistance to a Realistic Approach

It is not uncommon to find spouses who resist suggestions advocating realistic self-concepts on the ground that these imply too optimistic a view of the self. They maintain that Christian doctrine calls for a negative attitude. Man, they say, has no good in him whatever; he is totally depraved and can do nothing good.

One husband alienated himself from his wife by saying that the sins he committed could not be helped. "After all," he said, "the Bible says we are all depraved and sinful. Our entire personalities are filled with sin; there is nothing worthy in us." The tone of his voice, his facial expressions, and his subsequent explanation of his concept of the "depravity of man" all pointed to an intellectual justification of his behavior.

[2]See Seward Hiltner's volume, *Constructive Aspects of Anxiety* (with K. Menninger).

Evidence pointed to the fact that the husband was in fact a Christian, but his theology was faulty. When a Christian declares that there is *nothing* of worth in his being, he is denying the presence of the Holy Spirit in his life. A Christian must accept the fact that his body is the "temple of the Holy Spirit" (I Cor. 6:19) and is characterized by *some* good, if nothing more than the Spirit living within him. Also, if there is an *intention* to do good (even though one fails to do it), the motivation behind the intention must contain some factor of goodness or it could never have been purposed at all. To believe otherwise deprives man of all freedom of will and leads toward making God responsible for man's sinful behavior.

This client's faulty theological thinking regarding the nature of man's depravity had to be modified. In much of Protestant theology, he was informed, total depravity implies that original sin touches all the dimensions of man's being. It does not mean that each part is *thoroughly* permeated with sin. Berkhof has said that "total depravity" does not imply that every man is as thoroughly depraved as he can possibly become, but does indicate that the inherent corruption *extends* to every part of man's nature.[3] To hold the view that sin thoroughly and completely controls man is to vitiate the grace and power of God in His creation activity and to exclude any element within man that could respond to God's love.

Any effort, therefore, to produce a realistic self-image should include a description of *both* the positive and the negative dimensions in human personality.

Complimenting One's Spouse

If a mate refuses to accept genuine compliments on the grounds that he has no good within him, he simply reinforces his distorted concept of his own nature. Since any

[3]*Systematic Theology*, pp. 246f.

such attitude opposes reality, it is bound to create personality problems sooner or later. The wife or husband must evaluate the extent to which a negative image exists in the spouse, and then help that partner move toward a realistic image of himself through genuine compliments and other means.

Some of the questions that help assess negative traits are: Does the spouse think about himself negatively in large part? How long has he thought about himself this way? How intensely does he perceive himself as lacking positive qualities? What family and interpersonal factors presently operating would lead him to maintain the image he holds of himself? On the basis of the answers to questions like these, the length and the kind of compensatory experiences required to offset any possible negative image may be projected.

Stan came from a family that believed man is completely and totally sinful. Nothing that man did was good, or if man did carry out acceptable behavior it was only due to the "grace of God." Perhaps this theological position would have been satisfactory, except that it was unclear to all of the children, including Stan. When the parents spoke about Stan, it was never in an appreciative way, for, after all, anything that he did which was acceptable was not of his doing, but of God's.

Moreover, the parents felt a responsibility (and rightly so) to bring Stan and the other children up in the "admonition of the Lord." The problem, however, was that the concept of an "ideal child" was constantly before them as a model toward which they wanted their children to move. Because Stan could not measure up to perfection as expressed in the "ideal child," he was constantly criticized.

The result of all this was a highly negative self-image—a child who saw himself seldom, if ever, as a worthwhile human being but always as one who fell short of being an acceptable and praiseworthy individual.

When Stan married, his wife found that, no matter how sincere her compliments about his good qualities, he countered with a statement to the effect that it was not really he who had developed these, and how much *better* he could and should be. Constantly he demeaned himself by comparing his personality with a perfect image. When he discussed his contribution to the life of his church, he depreciated himself just as his parents had done when he was a child, saying it was not he that was able to do these things, but God.

Only after some time was Stan willing to accept himself as a person and recognize that *he*—indwelt by God, to be sure, but still *he, himself*—was characterized by good qualities. Slowly he developed a realistic self-concept and a sense of self-acceptance. He began to think more positively about himself and to compliment others when it was justified and appropriate. And he began to express appreciation to his wife when she deserved it, as the Bible suggests (Prov. 31:28). Life was now happier and more enjoyable for him, though he knew he still had problems. He knew he was not perfect. But he was able to accept himself as he previously was unable to do. He began to have an attitude toward himself that was not unlike that which God holds toward his children, loving them and *accepting them just as they are.*[4]

Clinically, it has been found that the longer a person has held a negative self-concept the more repeated must be the stress on his positive traits for him to approach a realistic view of himself. If he has had extremely hostile attitudes toward himself, the need for strong emotional experiences to reinforce the positive qualities identified in his personality will be greater. The aim, of course, is to counteract the unrealistic negative self-image with positive experiences until self-perceptions are reasonably realistic.

[4]The doctrine of justification includes God's *acceptance* and love of his children in their present position. This is to be distinguished from the doctrine of sanctification which deals with God's encouragement of his children *to grow* and to improve their Christian life.

How does a husband or wife determine that a spouse has achieved such a realistic self-concept? One helpful way is to encourage self-disclosure in the marriage relationship, so that both will be free to discuss their observations and insights. If this is done with an attitude of accepting love, the need for defending one's image or personality will be minimal. The information that comes out in this type of relationship will be a sufficient indicator of how much realism a person has attained.

Occasionally, a mate will object to a spouse's compliments by quoting, "One ought not to think more highly of himself than he ought to think" (Rom. 12:3). But the problem is that he thinks more *lowly* of himself than he ought to think. The intent of this Scripture verse is to lead an individual into a grateful and realistic self-view. It certainly is *not* advocating a depreciating, debasing attitude toward the self. The whole tenor of Scripture points to the peace, assurance, confidence, and security that God provides for His children. God does not want His children to debase themselves, but to rejoice in their position and standing in His eyes—accepted, loved, supported, and encouraged.

Understanding the nature of personality should be the basis, of course, for the choice of methods used in building realistic and healthy self-images.

A husband and wife came for therapy since both were having extramarital affairs and recognized their desperate need for help. They saw themselves as completely sinful. Both needed to see themselves more realistically, but each had to be treated in a different way.

The wife needed direct statements about some of her good qualities. For example, she was repentant and had wanted to break off her unhealthy relationship with the other man from the beginning—demonstrating some goodness, however minimal it might have been. This positive quality was stressed and encouraged.

The husband, however, was totally opposed to any direct statements about his "good self." His attitude, developed during childhood with his mother, was to oppose any statement made. He enjoyed playing "lawyer" and was always ready and willing to take the opposite side of any subject.

The approach that served best in working with him was indirect and relatively neutral. Questions were asked about his work, his educational achievements, and his previous involvement in church work. The principle was to ask questions with no overt connotation of "good," but which required him to reveal some of the positive things he had done in the past.

Some of the questions that were used were the following: "You have supported the family throughout your married life, is that correct?" "You have completed college?" "For some years you taught Sunday school?" "You have taken the children to church each Sunday since you discontinued attending church yourself?" It would have aroused resentment in this particular individual if a moral value had been attached to these questions. To have said, "One *good* thing you have done is to support your family throughout your marriage," would have undoubtedly brought the reply: "Oh, I didn't do *nearly* what I should have done. *Other men* do much more for their families." Such a response would simply have reinforced his already poor self-concept and heightened his negative attitude toward himself. But by being exposed to indirect references to his good self and being allowed to draw the conclusion that there was some residual goodness in him, he was eventually led to greater self-acceptance, improved moral behavior, and resumption of church attendance with his wife and children.

What he had been led to do indirectly was to think realistically about both his good and bad traits, so that he perceived himself as wrong in his extramarital behavior, but not so completely sinful as to be beyond the point of divine help or forgiveness. He could see that he had *some* qualities that his wife and family appreciated (his support of them, his sense of responsibility in taking the children to Sunday school, his educational attainment, and his former involvement at church).

His experience was not unlike that of others who feel that God's love and forgiveness are unavailable to them. Such people are interpreting the Scriptures by their feelings and disregarding the fact that God's Word stands true no matter what feelings a person may have. This does not alter the fact that we must understand and help people where they are and deal with their feelings if these interfere with their attainment of truth and realism. As a matter of fact, one of the goals of personal development ought to be achieving realism at the emotional level. It is not enough to develop a realistic self-image at the intellectual level only: one cannot just *think* right but must eventually *feel* right, since man is a unity.

A well-balanced and total program for changing negative self-images should include, therefore, positive intellectual, emotional, and other experiences so that an acceptable and healthy self-concept can be attained.

The Intellectual Mate

Husbands and wives should recognize that highly intellectual spouses have usually trained themselves to think in terms of opposites, sometimes because "seeing both sides of the issue" is intellectually stimulating to them, other times because of a family background in which they could preserve their own identity in childhood only by being oppositional. Either way, a spouse with this tendency will have a hard time establishing a healthy self-image.

A spouse has a choice of two methods in dealing with

this kind of oppositional personality type—silence or agreement. The "silent" approach allows him to draw his own positive (or at least nonnegative) conclusions.

Husband: "I'm always doing things wrong."
Wife (silence)
Husband (thoughtfully): "Well, perhaps it isn't as bad as it seems" (seeing the positive side).

Or, with a person who possesses a strong ego and is not easily discouraged:

Husband: "I'm always doing things wrong."
Wife (in agreement): "Yes, dear, it really does happen that way, doesn't it?"
Husband (in typically oppositional style): "Oh, I don't know that it's that bad" (seeing something of the positive side).

There are some individuals who evidence a superior intelligence, but are extremely pliant and conforming by nature. It is best for the spouse of such a person to avoid the tactic of agreeing with him in the hope that he will take an opposing view. Generally speaking, such persons have insufficient emotional resources for developing and holding such a view, so that they frequently adhere to the expressed and prevailing sentiment, whatever it is. Such a case calls for stating the facts carefully, allowing the person to draw the positive conclusions himself. Showing an interest in his accomplishments, providing help on projects of a positive nature, and genuinely showing appreciation of any constructive programs that he initiates will all be helpful.

In any case, one must understand his spouse fairly well in order to decide which method will produce satisfactory results.

Proper Use of Criticism

Is there a place for constructive criticism? The best answer is that there are many places, but the method employed should be perceived as helpful by the person criticized. If he interprets the comments negatively, as an attack on him, the criticism cannot have constructive effects, regardless of its intention. Two general principles must be kept in mind for constructive criticism that promotes, rather than hinders, the development of healthy self-images. First, one should not focus on the *wrong* way a thing is being carried out. Avoid saying things like "That's not the way to do it, let me show you how"; or "There *must* be a better way than that." Such statements tend to lower the person's self-esteem and build a wall of resistance to any help offered. No one likes to be thought incapable of doing a job or picking the right method for it. A more promising approach is for the spouse to suggest how something might have been done differently, but not necessarily better. The decision about which method is *better* is not stated by the helpful spouse, but left to the other person. He decides what method to use since he can best tell what is suited to his personality and resources. This will enhance his feeling of independence and contribute to his recognition of his own personal identity with its unique qualities, skills, and ways of thinking.

The second principle is to avoid making negative comments about the individual or his personality. Resentment-producing remarks like the following should be avoided: "How stupid can you be?"; "Anyone else with an ounce of common sense would have done something else"; "There you go, blundering again." If a wife or husband has made an error, he or she probably regrets it; no one enjoys making mistakes. It would be better to say, sympathetically, something like "It must be terribly disappointing to have that work out the way it did"; or "It must have been a difficult experience to go through"; or "It must have hurt you deeply to have him say that." This permits the individual to say, "Yes, it was disappointing, but I think I'll survive. Perhaps next time it will be different." Thus he has picked up hope and encouragement from the understanding extended.

Words and Emotions

Husbands and wives should recognize and avoid emotionally charged words that greatly aggravate a spouse. One may not object in the midst of a heated discussion to being called "uncooperative," "hard to get along with," or "difficult," but if he is constantly referred to as "stupid," "ignorant," "idiotic," or some similarly degrading term, the repetition will eventually arouse resentment, block communication, and destroy any positive self-concepts.

Obviously, the "trigger" words—words that set off hostile emotions—should be identified and eliminated from one's vocabulary early in the marriage. The longer they have been used, the more vigilance and continuous evaluation of words and thoughts required to screen them out systematically from one's regular vocabulary.

Insufficiency of Love

It is easy to say that, if spouses only loved each other enough, problems like those we have discussed in this chapter would take care of themselves, and realistic and healthy self-images would automatically develop. Experience has shown that for the vast majority of couples this is not true. Love can provide the *motivation* for working out problems, improving communication, and building healthy self-images, but it does not solve problems by itself. Hard work, knowledge, and determination are necessary for solving the problems of life. Integral to the solution of many problems of living is the need for a married couple to provide mutual help in the development of wholesome self-concepts. It is necessary to remember that personality development does *not* end when one gets married and starts a family. There is a continuing need for a husband and wife to help each other throughout life in order to become the fully developed persons they are intended to be.

Summary

1. One ought not to have an overly optimistic nor an overly pessimistic view of himself for any prolonged period of time. A realistic self-concept should be the goal.
2. Those who assent to the doctrine of total depravity should recognize that this implies that each dimension of man's personality is affected by sin, but it does not preclude the possibility of some good in personality.
3. It may be necessary to put compensatory emphasis on positive personality factors in an individual who has held a negative self-concept for a long period until he attains a realistic picture which takes both the negative and positive factors into account.
4. Individuals who are very intelligent and those who enjoy "taking the opposite side of every issue" should avoid the tendency to reject compliments when these are sincerely and honestly given. To do so may only further reinforce unhealthy, negative self-images.
5. If constructive criticism is necessary, statements should be directed not at the person but at the *objects* involved or the *methods* used in the situation. Even then, the emphasis should be on how different methods or techniques might be employed, rather than on the defects of the method in use.
6. Exercising empathy with a disappointed mate by reflecting his moods will usually help one avoid negative criticism and relate to the mate constructively.

7. Emotionally charged words that "trigger" violent emotions should be identified and then carefully avoided.
8. If deep love is accompanied by an intelligent approach to building a marriage, healthy self-concepts and a stable marriage are far more likely to result. Love alone, though most important as a motivating force, is usually insufficient. Knowledge, determination, and a willingness to work diligently at problem-solving are also essential for realistic self-images and successful marriage.

4. Improving Communication

"How can I achieve happiness and satisfaction if my spouse refuses to communicate with me?" This is one of the questions a husband or wife most frequently asks when first seeking marital counseling.

Husbands complain that their wives simply will not discuss important family matters with them for seemingly unknown reasons. Wives complain also and wonder whether the so-called advantages of married life really outweigh the disadvantages when they feel such a lack of communication with their husbands.

One wife reported to her therapist, "My husband is an extremely fine conversationalist when he is at work and when we go out with a group of people, but if he is home alone with me he is the 'silent type,' and I don't know how much longer I can take it." Since she enjoyed conversing a great deal, she found it frustrating to be treated like this, and this frustration eventually turned into loneliness and depression.

Generally, we find that disappointment and disillusionment are the underlying causes of the breakdown in communication between husband and wife. Where there had previously been common plans and dreams, now there are only shattered hopes and deep despair. The need for communication, companionship, and sharing is still present, but the channels are all but closed. This is not the way marriage should be, nor is it the way God intended it to be. Man is created a social being, and solitude is not good for him. Married couples must recognize, however, that companionship involves different types of communication.

Types of Communication

There are many husbands and wives who have a strong desire to communicate with their spouses at an *intellectual level*. When a husband, for example, arrives at home after work, his wife, who has been with the children all day, may be eager for some adult, intellectual stimulation. There is no doubt that she loves her children; nevertheless, she looks forward to her husband's arrival, not only because of her love for him, but for the opportunity to talk to him on subjects of common interest.

Frequently, however, the husband comes home, mutters a few words of greeting, retires to his chair (perhaps in front of the television set) and opens up the evening paper. If his wife asks how things went at work, he ignores her or tells her he is too tired to talk and wants to be left alone until dinner is ready.

Now it may well be that nothing has happened at work that the husband feels is worth mentioning. But if he recognizes his wife's need for some kind of intellectual interaction, he will enter into conversation with her and relate some of the day's events, dull and boring though they may seem to him, thus meeting her intellectual need to maintain an active and growing mind.

A second level of communication is the physical. Jim was thirty-five and extremely angry. His wife, who was thirty, had refused him the normal number of sexual relationships for their age-group for several years. Their conversation with the therapist indicated a deficiency in their physical communication.

Jim: "This wife of mine has just about ruined our marriage because she is so frigid."

Wife: "All he ever thinks about is sex."

Jim: "That isn't true. I'm only interested in relations about three times a month."

Wife: "Well, there are other more important things that can be a demonstration of love, too. We both enjoy talking to each other, and I show him my love by my work around the house."

Jim: "But sex relations are important for me, I know that. Just to have her warmth and affection is what I crave. And I feel this most deeply in the sexual relationship, as I think I should."

For Jim, intellectual exchanges and the usual domestic indications of love (cooking, cleaning, and other housekeeping tasks) were not enough. There was a definite need to express love through the physical relationship. He was, therefore, terribly irritated with the way his marriage was working; as indeed most men would have been.

Theologically and psychologically, sexual intercourse is a necessary mode of communication by which spouses come to know each other in an exceptional way. It helps couples meet some of their needs at the deepest level of personality and express their real selves in a way that words cannot. It was this type of fellowship and communication that Jim missed.

> A very special kind of knowing goes with sexual knowledge. The Old Testament actually describes sexual intercourse itself as a process of "knowing" . . . Adam "knew" Eve his wife (Gen. 4:1). But the same can be said of the woman with respect to the man. . . . If the sex act had been regarded merely as a

physical process, it surely would have been more natural to choose a physical symbol. . . . Obviously, there must have been an inner affinity between the act of sexual union and the act of knowing the other partner.[1]

A third level of communication is the *emotional.*

Bob found that his wife felt extremely insignificant and unimportant. He had a job loading trucks in the early morning, so he left home at 4 a.m. and finished his work for the day about 1 p.m. Instead of driving home after work, he spent most of the afternoon in a bowling alley, arriving home just in time for the evening meal and then retiring to bed immediately afterwards. After several such years of treatment, the wife began to feel neglected, because the most significant person in her life, her husband, did not take time to be with her. This eventually boiled over into bitterness and hostility.

The wife revealed to the therapist that if her husband had made her feel wanted and appreciated, thus feeding her emotional life, she would have been satisfied. One way he could have done this would have been by spending afternoons at home, caring for the yard and maintaining the house they were buying. In this way, they would have been working on a common objective, the care and upkeep of their property. Bob's presence at home, moreover, would have given her emotional satisfaction and a sense of self-esteem because someone important wanted to be with her and help her with the work around the house. This became, then, a therapeutic goal designed to help him move toward a different pattern of relating to his wife.

There are other types of communication, of course, but married couples must recognize these three if they expect to build a happy and satisfying marriage relationship.

[1] H. Thielicke, *Ethics of Sex,* pp. 66f.

Dealing with Boredom

After the first few years of marriage, husbands and wives often develop an apathetic attitude toward each other and lose interest in communicating.

A wife said about her lawyer husband: "All he ever wants to talk about is his law practice. It's the Jones case today and the Smith case tomorrow. Or it may be the dinner he had with some judge or the subject matter at a recent bar association meeting. But it's always some subject connected with his practice. I try to talk about these things with him, but I can't really contribute anything to his knowledge. All I can do is simply rehash his ideas in one form or another."

Her husband readily agreed. "Yes, I admit that I do get bored conversing with my wife. I can almost predict what she is going to say before she says it. She never seems to have any new ideas. She just isn't as interesting as she once was. About the only time that I ever become involved with her is when I am angry over her criticism of me."

This woman wanted to relate to her husband conversationally so that they might once again appreciate one another. Things had reached such an impasse that when they went out to dine in the evenings they would assume the appearance of a couple conducting a normal conversation. In actuality, however, they would look at each other and, not knowing what to say or discuss, start counting, beginning with one and going on until a smile would break out over their ridiculous behavior. This social facade was employed to give others the impression that all was well in their marriage.

Developing a new conversational style between husbands and wives who have become bored with each other requires a great deal of effort and sympathetic understanding. Tournier has said in this regard:

There are men who are like mysterious islands. They protect themselves against any approach. They no longer express themselves, nor do they take a stand on anything. When their wife consults them on something important, they hide themselves behind their paper. They look deeply absorbed. They answer without even looking up, in a tone impersonal, anonymous, and vague, which excludes all argument.[2]

Couples who try to break an ineffective communication pattern after several years of relative failure will find two rather formidable resistances. First, any attempt at conversation may appear to be unreal and lacking in authenticity, thus discouraging the effort at a program of improvement. Second, they may fail to sympathize enough with each other in this effort. After several days of experimenting, they may become skeptical and critical of the whole venture and regress to the noncommunicative patterns of the past. Under such circumstances a couple must recognize that this type of change in behavior will appear artificial at first and that it will take time to become natural and fixed. Patience, understanding, and a sense of humor are obviously called for, since behavioral changes in spouses married for a considerable length of time usually require a great deal of sympathetic reinforcement for months and sometimes years. The development of a skill like conversing together takes a great deal of time and practice. As time passes, the artificiality and sense of inauthenticity will begin to disappear.

One couple learned to use humor in overcoming both their sense of boredom with each other and their anger over a disorganized house routine. He used to order her to clean up certain areas of the house, and she would respond with silence. She attempted to instruct him about putting things in order around the house, and he would refuse to respond. Neither could tolerate the attitude of the other. Their unwillingness to communicate about household

[2]*To Understand Each Other*, pp. 16f.

duties was symptomatic of most of their other relationships. Eventually, an agreement was reached which made each feel comfortable. They discussed "their" home. For several months, they were instructed to say to each other: "*We* really need to clean our house up now, don't we?" This usually involved laughter because they knew that the suggestion had come from their therapist. A similar approach was used in attacking several problems in other areas of their life. In each case, they found that a sense of humor was absolutely essential if they were to avoid making charges of insincerity, artificiality, and phoniness and to recognize the situation for what it was—an effort to make life happier for both through an experiment in improved communication.

A helpful step toward improving techniques of communication is to set up an extensive program of reading newspapers and magazines in order to become more knowledgeable about current events and areas of mutual interest. For example, the attorney's wife previously mentioned might have located articles that dealt with legal matters and read crucial passages from them to her husband in an interesting and enthusiastic tone of voice. Or she might have asked her husband his opinion about the legal dimensions of a court case that had been reported in the newspapers for some time. Not every husband is interested in providing opinions for his wife to react to, but many feel complimented when their wives ask for advice based on their knowledge and experience.

Playing the "devil's advocate" sometimes helps stimulate conversation between spouses, though it frequently leads to bickering. There are some situations in which negative communication is preferable to none at all. A wife and husband under such circumstances might take opposing views and thereby create an interesting conversation. This approach should be used with caution, however, or it may result in an unconscious and irritating habit of opposing one's partner on all subjects simply for the sake of conversation.

Initiating a Conversation

A wife or husband may start a conversation with a question, a statement, or an exclamation. But whatever method is used, there must be some *feeling* connected with it. A dull voice seldom brings an enthusiastic response. For example, the wife may ask her husband in an excited tone of voice, holding up the newspaper for him to see: "Were you looking for a good sale on tires, honey? How does this sale look to you?" Or she may make a statement, proudly, such as, "Johnny's ball team won their game this afternoon. Isn't that wonderful!" Or she may exclaim, enthusiastically, "What a beautiful day! Let's go and do something together as a family." If there is a brightness and positive quality in the tone of voice, the chances for a pleasant response are much greater, and a conversation is more likely to start.

Should none of the above approaches prove effective, the "oppositional" method might be employed. If one spouse favors increased taxes, the other takes the opposing view. If one says it is best to elect a Republican candidate, the other points up the qualities of his Democratic opponent. The outcome of such an approach may be communication. It may also produce, as a fringe benefit, helpful information to guide their voting.

Focusing on Feelings

Successful encouragement of conversation requires a person to note the feeling or emotional tone his spouse uses in his statements. The attorney we have been discussing may come home and say to his wife, "Well, I won the Smith case in court today, and it certainly was a good experience for me." Now if his wife responds by saying something like "How long was the jury out?", she is simply asking for information, and not reflecting or inquiring about his feelings. It would be better for her to sense his feeling of satisfaction and reply with admiration, "I'm sure Mr. Smith was very happy with your work. You always do well. What did he say after it was all over?" This would show her admiration for her husband's efforts and cause him to reflect further on Smith's gratefulness, thus reinforcing a positive feeling and perhaps evoking additional conversation.

The husband who arrives home after a disappointing day at work may be encouraged to talk if he is met by a wife who can recognize his discouragement by such clues as his words, tone of voice, or the look on his face. If she says something like "I know how much you have given of yourself at work. It certainly must be discouraging at times"—in other words, if she tries to feel within herself the same as her husband, she thereby provides help, but does not eliminate the possibility of positive moods later in the evening. Reflecting as accurately as possible a spouse's moods and feelings promotes conversation, since most persons wanting to discuss their inner thoughts seek those who demonstrate understanding. And the person who is sympathetic, or even better, who can identify with another's feelings, is the person with whom such an individual usually will converse.

Interpersonal Relationships and Feelings

Since most persons are interested in the emotions of other people, it is possible to take almost any subject concerned with the feelings of fellow workers, friends, or relatives and discuss it interestingly. For example, presenting mere facts or plans connected with a program may not elicit sufficient interest for a conversation, because facts and plans as such may be completely devoid of emotion. But if the *emotions* of the people planning a program are discussed, the degree of interest will usually be much greater.

Suppose a husband comes home from work with the news that the boss has accepted a proposal he made. A wife may respond in a matter-of-fact tone by asking "What steps were involved in getting the boss to accept your proposal?" But a better approach would be for her to inquire about co-workers' feelings. She could say, enthusiastically, "Wonderful! Were the other men in the office as happy as I imagine the boss was about it?" The "feeling" words used in the latter type of response were "wonderful" and "happy." The former response contained no "feeling" words at all.

If she had used the first response, the wife would have missed an opportunity to create conversation. For her to focus on the nature of the proposal or the time taken in drawing it up or its length, instead of on the feelings of the workers, would be to invite the husband to respond with an apathetic attitude. For example, none of the following questions that the wife might have asked contain a "feeling" word: "What was the subject of the proposal?" "How much time did it take to work it out?" "How many pages did the proposal cover?" There is no focus on the feelings of the people involved. Thus conversation can be thwarted before it has a chance to begin.

Clinical experience has shown that when feelings receive special attention, they are powerful motivating factors for stimulating conversation and discussion. The psychological fact behind this is that persons need approval and appreciation. Both of these needs are fulfilled through the expressions of other persons. When a wife exclaims, "Wonderful! Were the other men in the office as happy as I imagine the boss was about it?" her husband feels that his wife not only approves of his work but actually admires his skill and ability, not only as an employee, but as a husband and a person as well.

Under these conditions, it is to be expected that he will feel more positively toward himself and experience a freedom and an openness that spontaneously create a climate conducive to pleasant conversation. He might respond: "Yes, the men at work congratulated me and seemed very enthusiastic about the whole thing. As a matter of fact [here the husband becomes so emotionally interested in the subject because of his wife's interest that he decides to elaborate on it], it looks as though this will be just the first of several projects which the boss wants me to work on. And are the fellows in my department enthusiastic! They not only want to work on these projects but they are also willing to provide any support they can, even to the point of doing extra work if it's necessary in order to move the program along toward the deadlines the company has set up. . . ."

Notice that the response of the husband has been in terms of feelings: "the men *congratulated* me" (which his wife had also done in her appreciative tone of voice using the "feeling" words of "wonderful" and "happy"); ". . . the first of several projects which the boss *wants* me to work on . . . ." Thus, an effort to focus on moods and feelings tends to evoke greater desire for conversation.

Reflecting Feelings and Mood Patterns

Reflecting a mate's feelings is very helpful in creating an atmosphere favorable to conversation. Phoniness, artificiality, and all that lacks genuineness, however, should be avoided. There must be a *true* desire to help the other person by mirroring his emotions and moods. St. Paul speaks of this as "rejoicing with those who rejoice and weeping with those who weep" (Rom. 12:15). It is a genuine desire to help another person through "feeling with him" his experiences of life. Psychologists refer to this as empathy. One of the results of an empathic relationship is that a person senses he is better understood because someone feels what he feels. Along with this understanding comes a confidence that if he expresses himself he will not be ridiculed or criticized, but will find someone who is helpful, constructive, and emotionally supportive. Communication involving a disclosure of one's inner thoughts and sentiments is much easier when one need not fear ridicule or misunderstanding, and consequently there is no need to withhold one's thoughts or feelings.

In seeking to reflect feelings, one should note a spouse's voice and his facial expressions. Underneath, of course, there must be a deep and loving desire to enter into his world with all of the risks that are involved. *Complete* identification with the moods and feelings is not recommended, however, for this would destroy one's own identity and would in fact work against the development of a helping relationship. If a wife becomes as angry as her husband at a situation, she might reinforce both his hostility and hers and aggravate the relationship. The reflection of feeling should be carried out to different degrees in different people, but never to the point of a complete loss of identity on the part of the one seeking to help and understand.

If a mate has experienced sorrow or deep disappointment and he is speaking in a low tone of voice, softly and more slowly than usual, the spouse's response should be in the same manner. "It must have been a great disappointment to you. I'm so sorry. Is there anything that I can do?" are statements that can give a great deal of understanding and reassurance, especially when spoken in a tone of voice that reflects the spouse's. "Regardless of the technique used, all studies of adults thus far reported in the literature agree that emotional meanings can be communicated accurately by vocal expression."[3]

Facial expressions are also highly significant in reflecting

[3] J. R. Davitz, *The Communication of Emotional Meaning,* p. 23.

feelings and fostering communication between individuals.[4] This is exemplified in the following incident:

Husband (sitting in the car with his wife puzzling over a road map): "This is certainly a hard one to figure out."

Wife (reflecting his concern by seriously studying the map with him, perhaps frowning): "It does seem to be a very difficult map to read." (She says this only if she can be genuine in her statement; otherwise she would remain silent.)

Husband (sensing that his wife feels along with him): "Yes, and not only that, but the legend at the bottom of this map is incomplete. I'll do the best I can, but I'll need you to look at the other half of this map. Maybe the two of us can get this worked out."

Some wives, however, would have stifled any such opportunity for conversation by failing to use a similar or equivalent mood, but would instead have expressed disgust in face and voice by looking angry and saying, "If you can't read it, let's forget it" or (with sarcasm), "Don't tell me you're having trouble reading that map *again*!" Critical statements and feelings such as these create emotions of anger and resentment and often produce silence or a sharp critical comment in return, either way blocking good communication.

The nonverbal factors, therefore, that foster communication (using similar tones of voice, facial expressions, etc.) should be given attention as well as the words that are spoken. Verbal and nonverbal modes of communication should always reinforce each other so that spouses feel understood and constructively helped by their partners in every way. When this is done, the hope for a truly satisfying life of companionship comes much closer to actual realization.

[4]*Ibid.*, p. 13.

Summary

1. Without communication regarding the nature of their marital problems and needs, husbands and wives cannot arrive at satisfactory solutions.
2. Males and females are created so that they will provide companionship in marriage for each other, but this goal is blocked if communication is ineffective or nonexistent.
3. Many mates require that intellectual, emotional, or physical needs (or a combination of these) be met in order for them to maintain a satisfying life of communication.
4. Vocal enthusiasm is useful in initiating a conversation if different approaches are used (question, statement, exclamation).
5. If a mate "listens" for the feeling or mood expressed in the tone of voice of a spouse, comments relating to the mood tend to promote communication and conversation.
6. Focusing on the feelings of friends, relatives, or colleagues of one's mate is helpful in creating interesting conversation.
7. Since most persons tend to limit their conversation if the other party is unsympathetic, it is best to reflect a person's mood or emotions in an understanding and genuine fashion when speaking, so that he feels comfortable in continuing with the topic of conversation.

5. Defining Authority

The Issue of Competitiveness

One of the great social issues today is the question of equality of opportunity between the sexes. Equal opportunity has long been sought by women, and its realization comes closer with each passing year. Equality, of course, implies that men and women will be competing increasingly for job openings and for advancement in many areas of society. Nathan Ackerman, commenting on this development, has said, "The competitive aspect of the relations between the sexes has become a virtual battleground because of the associated connotations of superiority and inferiority. This is superfluous and harmful."[1] It is very likely that this competitive attitude will continue to spread to all areas of life, including that of authority within marriage.

Though a competitive spirit may be economically healthy in the business world, there is a very real question whether it is appropriate in the home. The uncertainty that it produces in husbands and wives is one of the chief causes of marital unhappiness. Competitiveness is seldom, if ever, conducive to a sense of warmth and affection; instead it tends to create anxiety, jealousy, anger, and a host of other emotions inimical to cultivating love. This being so, a couple must decide early in married life whether they wish to make their major goal one of warmth and love and cooperation or of selfish competitiveness.

[1] *Psychodynamics of Family Life*, p. 173.

More than one mate has implied from the very beginning of marriage that there would be competition for power and authority. In the beginning, this may involve physical tests of strength. If the husband wins these tests, his wife will probably conclude (perhaps unconsciously) that her husband is more capable than she when tasks involving strength are faced. But this may be only the first of a series of physical, social, psychological, emotional, and even religious experiences to determine who is the superior mate in the different areas of life. Additional tests for power in marriage may take the form of seriously competitive experiences in money management and in matters relating to sexual intercourse. After these and other experiences have made their impact—both conscious and unconscious—a couple may settle down to build their marriage based on the outcomes of the marital fighting that has gone on.

Perhaps the most unfortunate marriages are those in which husbands and wives keep on battling each other for authority in all areas of life even after it appears that settlements have been achieved. Such marital "wars" are likely to go on until the marriage is broken by divorce, separation, or death. This situation is far too common today, and it militates against the very institution of marriage. Beyond that, it tends to prevent husbands and wives from achieving any satisfaction from the attainment of personal and vocational goals, since so much time and energy are expended in marital struggles.

Underlying the desire for power is usually an unconscious pattern or image of what a marriage "ought to be." The husband may hold one view of what the marriage should be like and the wife another. Once the burden and responsibilities of marriage break in on them, each makes strong efforts to see his image of the "perfect marriage" become a reality. Tears, threats, promises, bargains, pleas, exploitations, and manipulations—all may be used in order to gain the desired authority and power to implement one's own personal end. Most of the maneuvers a spouse employs, however, may be entirely unknown to him until someone—his mate, another family member, or a therapist or counselor—points them out. In any case, the sooner he discovers the interpersonal tactics that he habitually uses, and identifies the ones that are jeopardizing his marriage, the more likely it is that something can be done about the situation.

The main thing a couple must recognize is that most husbands and wives are sincere in their desire to establish the plan that they feel is best for the marriage. Their struggle usually centers around the use of authority, that is, the right to put one's own plan forward for both to follow. If each partner is convinced that the other honestly wants what is best for the marriage, it becomes easier for them to discuss their mutual problems.

Undoubtedly, there are partners who are extremely egocentric and selfish and not at all interested in their mates' welfare. But clinical experience in working with married couples indicates that a conscious selfishness in regard to authority relationships is not a primary motivating force in most cases. Thus, it is best for married couples to assume from the beginning that spouses are interested in helping each other and are not *consciously* motivated by selfishness when differences occur in regard to matters of authority. If such motives do become evident and threaten the marriage, professional help is strongly advised.

Manipulation

One of the psychological insights generally overlooked by couples is that a spouse who *unknowingly* manipulates in order to gain authority may be engaging in a practice that can help a marriage. This does not imply that manipulation is recommended for improving marriages. But unconscious manipulating practices have been known to keep marriages intact until one or both partners attain greater understanding.

For example, the extrovert wife who feels that she cannot be happy without frequent social experiences may schedule dinners, parties, and other events as a means of gaining emotional satisfaction (and repressing thoughts of hostility toward her nonsocial husband). The husband is manipulated into social situations to which he is opposed. Yet his wife may know him well enough to realize that if he were given a choice between frequent social events or explosions of anger and hostility from her, he would opt for the former. In essence, the marriage is held together by a manipulating mechanism with which both appear to be in agreement. The wife hopes that in time her husband will begin to understand her many emotional needs. Efforts to satisfy personal needs, therefore, often result in manipulative behaviors, and only when spouses have gained enough insight into each other's needs is there progress toward the elimination of such practices.

What is unspoken—and usually unrecognized—in marriage, especially in the early years of married life, is that each transaction and agreement made between husband and wife helps establish rules of operation, many of which are the result of manipulation at the unconscious level. A wife may offer to stop nagging if the husband takes out an insurance policy. Or the husband bargains with his wife: "If you provide me with more frequent sex relations, you can furnish the bedroom any way you wish." Compromises involving unconscious manipulation usually become semi-permanent rules, governing matters like the formation of friendships, leisure activities, social and interpersonal relationships, child training, and religious activities.

Over the years, there will be conversations, discussions, and arguments focusing on personal needs in which considerable manipulation will occur. But manipulation ultimately militates against marital happiness:

> It is possible to manipulate the spouse by appealing to his sense of vanity, ego, self-esteem, or good judgment, but such mental trickery is easily found out and resented. Life cannot be a masquerade.[2]

Psychologists may be capable some day of spelling out in clear and precise terms the various needs of husbands and wives and then develop detailed programs according to which everyone can provide a sufficient level of satisfaction for his spouse and receive sufficient satisfaction in return. Until that time arrives, husbands and wives must guard against manipulating each other and seek to carry out a type of bargaining in which each person gives and receives enough to bring sufficient happiness and meaning to life. As we have been emphasizing, the preferred method will be one of openness and willingness to discuss mutual needs, especially the emotional and psychological ones, since these are not as obvious as are the physical.

One wife, for instance, was very reluctant to admit to her husband that she had an emotional as well as a physical need for sexual relations more often than once a month. His home background had been such that he had repressed all sexual thoughts under threat of punishment from his parents. He had carried this pattern of repression into marriage, a pattern that pictured sex as something to be ignored or controlled as much as possible.

As a result of her openness and refusal to manipulate her husband psychologically, they developed a frequency of sex relations more compatible with the needs of both.

Types of Rules in Marriage

To unravel many of the complex patterns of manipulation husbands and wives use requires identification of the factors underlying what we have called the rules of their

[2]E. L. Shostrom, *Man, the Manipulator*, p. 184.

marriage. Who makes up these rules? Who has the authority to decide how they are to be stated and defined? Are the terms to be used in formulating the rules to be defined by *Webster's Dictionary* or will uniqueness of definition be allowed? One wife said in despair:

"The marriage is ended. My husband said so. It's finished. I don't even know why we're here." When the husband was asked about this, he frowned and shook his head, "No, it isn't over, but it is close to being finished as far as I'm concerned. My only comment was that the marriage was finished, but that didn't mean it was ultimately finished."

The husband did not mean that the marriage was absolutely and completely dead when he used the term "finished." His wife had never been informed of this meaning of "finished"—*nearly* ended but not *absolutely* so. Her husband was not using a dictionary definition, but one of his own. He felt that he had a right to devise his own word meanings when making up the rules governing the marriage. Until his wife understood her husband's use of words, she had no hope for initiating even the slightest attempt at a reconciliation.

Not only are there rules to be established and principles for setting up such rules, but there must also be rules for settling differences. Some of these may be more emotional than rational. A wife, for example, may feel it unwise to surrender her interest in a particular matter unless her husband becomes extremely angry about it. Up to that point, she may feel that there is sufficient justification for holding to her position. On the other hand, a husband's criterion for deciding to "give in" to his wife may be that he must make adjustments in his thinking and actions and become more flexible once she begins to shed tears. In either case, the rule for settlement is not intellectual but emotional. If an attitude provokes anger or tears, then, and only then, should it be changed.

There are also rules for postponing arguments. The wife's sign may be a dead silence with no further interest in communication; the husband's sign turning his back and walking away. For either one to pursue an argument after the "signal" has been given might produce a serious blow-up between them.

Haley, in commenting on rule-making operations, says that

> the process of defining who is to make the rules in the marriage will inevitably consist of a struggle between any couple. The tactics in this struggle are those of any power struggle: threats, violent assault, withdrawal, sabotage, passive resistance, and helplessness or physical inability to do what the other wants. The struggle is by no means pathological; it only becomes pathological if one or the other spouse attempts to circumscribe the mate's behavior while indicating that he or she cannot help it.[3]

Some individuals believe that the solution to the problem of conflicting rules is to be reached by making the husband responsible for rule-making. Others take the view that there should be an absolutely equal relationship between husbands and wives, and that neither should assume the total responsibility for this task.

Head of the House

This brings us to the question whether there should be perfect equality between husbands and wives or whether one spouse should be more dominant in the relationship. Traditionally, the man has been the leader of the marriage and family unit in most societies. His greater ability to protect the family through physical strength, his lesser involvement in child care, and his greater opportunity for education have no doubt contributed to this condition. Whether man's desire to dominate and woman's to be submissive are inborn or acquired characteristics is a moot

[3]*Strategies of Psychotherapy*, p. 126.

question. That there are changes occurring in masculine and feminine authority relationships today is indisputable. With the means available for both family limitation and daily supervision of children in child-care centers, educational and job opportunities for women are greater than ever. Society, moreover, has established and equipped law enforcement personnel and agencies to protect the citizenry, so that the need for the physical strength of men in the home has been reduced markedly. As the woman receives more and more education and bears fewer and fewer children, and as technological and protective services improve, the man's position of authority will continue to be modified.

As a result of such changes, the woman more often than not sees herself as more independent but wonders whether she should be. The man, on the other hand, feels less and less secure, because his position as undisputed leader of the household is not as obvious as it once was.[4]

If the wife comes from a family in which the father was the dominant and authoritative parent, she will probably expect her husband to conform to this image. But she may be hesitant to surrender some of the independence that she learned to enjoy between the time she left her parents' home and marriage. What she may then be asking is that she enjoy the benefits of independent living, but that her husband bear physical and financial responsibilities in and around the home and prove himself worthy of exercising authority and leadership in each area of married and family life before she surrenders her independence. A husband may find himself, then, in a difficult position. Society expects him to be responsible for financial affairs and other family matters, but his wife seriously reduces his authority for carrying out such responsibilities. Indeed, when she assumes the attitude that her husband must "prove" his right to be the head of the house, *she* is

---

[4]See Ackerman's *Psychodynamics of Family Life,* especially chapter eight.

already the one in authority, because her husband's right to be leader depends on *her* approval. This is similar to a parent-child relationship in which the parent says to a child, "If you behave in such-and-such a way, I will let you do what you have asked." The one in authority, in the final analysis, is the one who controls and lays down the rules by which someone else must abide.

One wife in discussing her husband's interest in becoming the head of the home asked him, "In what ways have I stopped you from becoming the head of the house?" He politely answered by giving her several illustrations, and then turned and suggested that they put their heads together to find out how they could change things for the better. To this she replied, "You tell me what you have in mind, and I'll tell you if it will work," thus remaining in control of the situation.

This short dialogue characterized their entire relationship. He was always in a position of having to give answers to her questions, which she in turn would accept or reject. Seldom if ever did she permit him to ask questions of her. She was in command of the relationship and stood against any effort by him to become the head of the house until she was satisfied that he deserved such a position. Her position was that of judge; his of the defendant trying to convince the judge of the rightness of his case. Only after receiving help over a number of sessions were they able to work out between them a satisfactory set of authority relationships.

Sharing Authority

Most married couples will distribute authority out of sheer necessity, if for no other reason. There are simply too many responsibilities involved in normal married living to place all authority in the hands of one spouse. If the wife did not have the authority to buy the groceries, feed the children, purchase clothes, and perform a number of other duties, it would be intolerably difficult for a husband to attempt to fulfil these responsibilities and simultaneously carry on a full-time job. The husband, in turn, must have authority to decide on the type of job for which he feels best suited and equipped, and how he will assume responsibility for the financial affairs of the household (since the state usually holds the husband responsible for this area of life).

The vast majority of couples come to realize that sharing responsibilities and authority is the only efficient and satisfactory way for them to manage. Their relationship is a complementary one, in which each partner carries out those tasks and responsibilities for which he appears most capable. To be sure, there will be overlapping of responsibility, but the general understanding is that the areas of living will be divided between the spouses with each carrying certain responsibilities. The understanding, of course, is that if emergency assistance is required from the spouse it will be available.

On what basis is authority divided? Usually, the special knowledge or skills possessed by a spouse help determine the assignment of authority.

Other bases of authority are the laws of society and of God. Legally and socially, for example, the man in a family usually has the right to select his place of work and the location of the family residence. Theologically, he is designated in many passages in the New Testament as the head of the household. But any analysis of authority relationships described in the Bible reveals some very general guidelines for husbands as household heads and wives as helpmates. The injunction is always present that Christian authority must involve mutual respect and service to one another in love. In this regard Emil Brunner has said,

> The husband will not insist on his "rights" as leader, and the wife will quietly and willingly concede them to him; . . . indeed she will even secretly encourage her husband to exercise these rights; even the "emancipated" woman will do this, in so far as she has remained a woman.[5]

Karl Barth has written in the same vein, stating that the man should precede the woman, "taking the lead as the inspirer, leader and initiator in their common being and action." If there is a subordination of woman to man, it is only secondarily so: "This subordination of woman is primarily and essentially to the Lord and only secondarily and unessentially to man." "Woman is certainly not expected to make herself a slave or chattel of man."[6]

All this suggests that certain areas of life may be the responsibility of one partner and not the other. Such a division should not be arbitrary but should take into account the many physical, emotional, social, religious, and educational qualities and factors of the two personalities involved. As difficult and complex as this might be, the wife and husband are usually aware enough of their knowledge, skills, and abilities to allocate areas of responsibility in a fairly satisfactory manner.

For each responsibility a spouse assumes, he must have the authority to carry it out. It is unfair and unrealistic to expect a spouse to fulfil his responsibilities without providing sufficient authority for discharging the responsibilities.

Husband: "You know I am a hard worker and that I must have good meals every day. And that means a roast or some kind of steak at the evening meal all through the week."

Wife: "You give me so little money for food each week that it's impossible to have the kind of meals you want. And, furthermore, you said not to write any

---

[5] *The Divine Imperative*, p. 380.
[6] *Church Dogmatics*, III/4, 170, 172, 173.

checks. So how can I give you the kind of meals you want?"

What has happened here is that the husband expects his wife to be responsible for meals that include roasts or steaks each night, but he refuses to grant her the authority to write checks at the market, and he fails to provide her with sufficient money (which also represents authority in its own right). If she is a conscientious food buyer, he must grant her the authority to write checks for the food he insists must be on the table or give her the equivalent amount of money.

Another situation relates to budgeting:

Wife (arriving home from shopping): "Honey, look what I purchased at a real bargain at the department store" (showing a dress).

Husband (irritably): "You gave up trying to manage our money affairs and so I have attempted it. But if I'm going to carry this responsibility, then I must have the authority to control all expenditures. The budget simply says we cannot afford that dress at this time."

Wife (dejectedly): "I suppose I could return it. But it certainly was a bargain."

In this instance, the husband had taken the responsibility for balancing the family budget. His wife knew she should not purchase anything outside of the necessities. When she bought the dress on impulse, she was annulling his authority. Husbands and wives must learn that mutual cooperation and adequate respect for authority must be present if each is to carry out his tasks and responsibilities satisfactorily.

Once a couple is aware of the need to allocate responsibilities and authority, it may take no more than six months to a year to work out a properly functioning program. But this does not finish the task at all. As children are born, as additional schooling is required for keeping up with one's line of work, as critical changes occur, the respective areas of responsibility and degrees of authority must be re-evaluated and, if necessary, revised. If there is love, sincerity, and openness between spouses, they should be able to work through the division of authority and responsibilities whenever the need arises. It must, however, be a continuous evaluation, for marriages are like any social institution: changes and modifications in plans must be made periodically in order to adjust to the changing circumstances of life.

Challenges to Authority

How should a challenge to one's authority be handled? What are the various methods available for dealing with challenges from a spouse?

One way of responding is to *reinterpret* what appears to be a challenge. That is, seek to think the best about a mate, not the worst. Instead of being defensive or suspicious about a partner's motive, simply assume that there is no threat, but that the partner—like most wives and husbands—wants the best for the marriage. So it is helpful to respond in a way that aims at relieving any tension that may be present. For example, in answer to a statement dealing with finances:

Wife (complaining): "You're not handling the money for our marriage correctly at all."

Husband (changing quickly from a suspicious to a puzzled mood, assuming that his wife wants to help and not take over the authority for managing the money): "Well, if you have a suggestion, I'll be glad to consider it. I know I'm not perfect. What did you have in mind?"

In this example, the husband recognizes his suspicious mood and, rather than accuse his wife of something that may not be true (that she wants to take over the financial affairs), he consciously changes his mood to one of puzzlement because she may well want to help him, even though she is critical. He retains his authority by stating that *he* will decide whether her suggestion is a good one. In this way, he is open to creative and helpful ideas from his wife, but does not interpret her remark as a challenge to give up his authority.

A second way for a spouse to face such a challenge is to *take special note of the emotional factor.* In the case described above, the husband might have reflected his wife's concern and said, "I'm worried about this too. I, too, am upset over our finances. And I've told myself I *must* get this budget balanced." The advantage of this approach is that she will tend to be less anxious if she sees that his attitude is one of serious concern, as hers is, implying that he is highly motivated to solve the problem confronting them.

A third way involves *focusing on the apparent intention* of the statement and confronting it as a challenge. Using this method, the husband might ask his wife, "Are you saying you would rather do the budgeting and book work? Is *that* what you are suggesting?" By asking a question of this nature and bringing the issue into the open, it is possible for him to retain the authority for keeping the responsibility or transferring it to her if necessary. "All right," he may say, "I have taken another look at my schedule and I can see I don't have the time for doing a good job. I'm giving, or delegating, it to you. Let's see how you do with it." In this method of handling a challenge, the individual retains the right to decide whether to give the job up or not. The alternative would likely be that of a heated argument in which the wife embarrasses the husband, complains about the poor job he is doing, lowers his self-esteem, and perhaps convinces him to give up the job, thus taking authority from him against his will.

If the husband retains the right of decision, he can then use the technique of delegation, as in the above example. He may delegate a responsibility to his wife because he does not have sufficient time, or because he is not technically equipped to handle the particular job, or because he needs to give himself to more important matters. All of these reasons for delegating responsibilities are common in the business world, and they are no less justified within the home. It is possible, in our day, that a wife might possess certain highly developed skills as a result of her educational or work background. For example, many wives have gained bookkeeping experience and make excellent money managers. If a husband assigns or delegates this to his wife, he still retains a position of authority, just as an employer does when he delegates the keeping of financial records to an accountant in his firm.

These, then, are several ways for handling threats to authority without necessarily arousing defensive or hostile attitudes. Generally, it is best to try the first method suggested, and move to the other methods only if the first fails to work. To start with the last method is not usually advisable, since it tends to foster resistance and needless anger in many situations. Experience has shown that, when people are suspected of negative motives when none is actually present, they tend to become resistant and hostile because their motives have been impugned.

Children and Authority Relationships

Ultimate authority for family plans should be placed in the hands of one person, according to those concerned with the administration of social institutions. If a family, moreover, follows the biblical view of authority, in which the husband is the ultimate authority, a unified family existence should be relatively assured. But that authority must be used to serve others, not for self-aggrandizement. The husband should seek to exercise his authority with a sense of responsibility in an attitude of love. Also, an attitude of equality before God should pervade the marital relationship. But if an impasse develops between a husband and wife in connection with some matter, if they simply cannot agree on something crucial to the well-being of the family, ultimate responsibility and authority should reside with the husband. As Thielicke has stated:

> At this point where a choice simply *has* to be made and where the exceptional character of a borderline situation prevails, a theological ethics cannot abstain from declaring, in line with the tradition of Christendom based upon the Holy Scriptures, that the father holds the final decision. Though it is true that the New Testament does not recognize any spiritual subordination of the wife to the husband (Gal. 3:28; Eph. 5:23; I Pet. 3:1) . . . it nevertheless upholds this subordination in the earthly affairs of marriage.[7]

In all likelihood, the children in such a family will avoid much confusion over authority relationships and will recognize that both parents are to be respected and obeyed, with the ultimate authority residing in the father (although he may delegate authority and responsibility of many kinds to his wife).

Since children, however, tend to exploit differences between fathers and mothers, parents should discuss matters of disagreement between themselves or in a formal family council so that a consistent authority structure and pattern of conduct is developed. This makes it difficult for children to play one parent against another and for one parent to undermine the other, thereby producing in the children a loss of respect for their primary authority figures (their parents), and for authority itself. Whether parents discuss things privately or in a family council, the understanding should be that the father is the final arbiter

[7] *The Ethics of Sex,* p. 158.

if violent disagreement should occur. He must, however, be willing to accept responsibility for any failure that results from his decisions. Ultimate responsibility, therefore, should automatically accompany the exercise of ultimate authority.

Words and Actions

Civil courts distinguish between the use of words and the use of action or physical force. Authority manifests itself in both of these forms at one point or another in our society. It is generally accepted today that physical force should be avoided and arguments settled through discussion rather than physically aggressive action. There should be no exception to this rule. Couples in the heat of an argument or discussion may not reason well, and only if the ban on physical contact is absolute and total will it be followed at such times.

> Our fight training outlaws physical violence . . . even though a tongue lashing may hurt more than physical violence, a physical fight between adults constitutes criminal assault and places anyone who switches from verbal to physical blows at a great disadvantage. He becomes a target of shame and condemnation and may even provide the victim with an excuse to exit and "win" a divorce.[8]

There was a time when many wives would tolerate minor physical mistreatment. Today, wives will not accept such treatment. The best rule, then, is to use words for settling disputes, not actions or physical force. In the final analysis, physical force is simply a way of communicating some fact, but it seldom, if ever, solves a problem satisfactorily. Slapping, spanking, hitting, twisting of arms, and the like may have been reluctantly and resentfully accepted in former times; these are no longer acceptable

[8]George Bach, *The Intimate Enemy*, pp. 111f.

today. The vast majority of people are well educated, and there is no reason why difficulties cannot be handled through discussion. Clinically speaking, virtually all efforts by spouses to settle disputes through the use of physical force fail. They aggravate, rather than settle, problems in the marriage. There is utterly no reason why discussion of problems cannot be sufficient, in view of the level of education that has been attained by most husbands and wives. The day of physical force is, for all practical purposes, gone. And the more husbands and wives resort to the use of reason and discussion for the solution of their problems, the more their children will tend to move away from the use of physical force and use reason and discussion themselves for working through their own problems.

Summary

1. Complementarity, rather than competitiveness, should characterize marriage relationships.

2. The married person should seek to identify the images of authority that he has derived from his background, rigorously examine each one, and then, through mutual study and discussion with his spouse, seek to establish lines of authority (and responsibility) consonant with his intelligence, sex, talents, skills, and experience.

3. When dealing with authority relationships, it is best to assume at the beginning that one's spouse is not seeking an advantage, but is primarily interested in what is best for the marriage. Otherwise, the suspicion of motives will tend to block any possible progress.

4. Although unconscious manipulation of one spouse by another is generally undesirable, it is not always a threat to a marriage. Spouses have been known unconsciously to manipulate circumstances for the general welfare of all in the marriage and family. *Con-*

tinuous and *conscious* manipulation, however, eventually militates against the marriage relationship.

5. One of the most difficult problems to settle is how to decide on the principles for making rules by which to live. Couples should thoroughly understand, therefore, the general basis underlying the rules of marriage relationship if effective communication is to result.

6. Spouses should seek to understand the meanings of the words that their partners employ. A statement that seems to endanger the very existence of a marriage may be made with a completely different intention. Spouses are advised, then, to seek clear elaborations of words, phrases, and sentences that are difficult for them to accept emotionally.

7. Specialists in the administration of social institutions have found that social units of two or more persons must have a single individual who exercises ultimate authority if confusion is to be avoided. Many clinical and theological data reinforce the concept that the male should serve as head of the family, and that he does so best if his authority is permeated by respect, love, and consideration for his wife and children.

8. Sharing of responsibilities is the generally accepted practice among married couples. Along with each of these responsibilities there should be sufficient authority to carry it out. To expect a person to carry a responsibility without adequate authority is impractical and self-defeating.

9. Challenges to one's authority may be handled by reinterpreting them as being nonthreatening, or by reflecting the moods connected with the statements of challenge (and making any needed changes which the challenges have brought to light), or by acknowledging the challenges and dealing with them directly. Challenges, however, are frequently a matter of testing limits without any desire to assume responsibility or the authority accompanying it.

10. Insofar as the husband carries the ultimate authority, he must also carry the ultimate responsibility for both successes and failures in the family.
11. Because children learn attitudes and behavior patterns through identification with their parents (or through parental figures), it is best for couples to think through carefully their own relationships so that sons and daughters will develop appropriate attitudes toward authority and authority figures.
12. Exercises of authority should involve verbalizations only. Physical mistreatment of spouses invariably blocks constructive relationships and creates deep-seated resentments that may affect happiness for prolonged periods of time.

6. Dividing Responsibilities

Influence of Parental Images

No marriage can be successful without shared responsibilities. A husband must assume his share of responsibility and the wife hers. The chances that a spouse will be motivated to assume his fair share of the obligations within the home are much greater if he has an image of his parents as responsible individuals. A recent study has shown that the example set by parents is a very significant factor in their children's assumption of responsibility. If the parents are responsible, the children, too, with very few exceptions, will be responsible.[1]

Although a husband and wife may acquire a sense of responsibility from the families in which they grew up, their *patterns* of responsibility may be considerably different. John and Ellen found this to be true in their case.

John's parents did not believe that wives should work outside the home, and so his father worked long, hard hours, and his mother assumed complete responsibility for the care of the house. When John's father arrived home, he rested and prepared himself for the next day; he seldom did any of the housework. Ellen's parents, on the other hand, tended to share housekeeping tasks on an almost equal basis, because each was employed.

[1]P. London and R. K. Bower, "Altruism, Extraversion, and Mental Illness," *Journal of Social Psychology*, Oct. 1968, pp. 19-30.

The images that John carried into marriage led to a pattern of living that precluded his doing any work around the house. In one sense, he had an irresponsible attitude toward household duties. Everything was left in Ellen's hands. But she brought entirely different images into the marriage. She not only sought employment outside the home, as her mother had done, but assumed that her husband would assist her in housekeeping as her father was accustomed to do for her mother. This was the picture indelibly and unconsciously stamped on her mind as to how wives and husbands cared for their homes.

Of course, each felt that his way of life was the "right" one. As a consequence, conflict, frustration, and bitterness were experienced by both—he refused to give his wife help, and she refused to do much of the work around their home, accusing him at times of being irresponsible.

In treating this problem, it was necessary to point out the influence of the parental images on their expectations of each other and the differences that actually existed between the situations of their parents and the one in which they found themselves. Satir has stressed this matter of parental influence:

> Our parents are our first teachers. We get our ideas of how to behave from what we see, what we experience and what we are told, and all this comes to us from our first teachers. You got your ideas from your respective first teachers.[2]

The need for John and Ellen to understand the place of family backgrounds in forming marital expectations and to recognize that their situation differed from that of their parents was emphasized as part of the program for working out their own pattern of domestic responsibilities.

[2]*Conjoint Family Therapy*, p. 124.

Encouraging Responsible Behavior

Often a deeply moving love for one's spouse may nurture the seed of responsibility within him and eventually lead to a satisfying division of labor in the marriage. But a continuous reinforcement of each act of responsibility is necessary through expressions of appreciation and praise if such behavior is to be cultivated.

It is at this point that one must recognize the need for identifying projects that are worthy of praise, which when it is given appropriately will not be rejected by one's mate.

Unfortunately, wives frequently overlook the commonly accepted tasks of men as being praiseworthy, just as men will often overlook those of women. A wife will say, "Oh well, he's *supposed* to work overtime whenever it's possible." Or, "When he mows the front lawn, it's for himself: it's his house, too." Husbands make the same error when they remark, "That's a wife's responsibility, she doesn't need any praise. I don't remember my father ever praising my mother for doing that kind of thing around the home." If she happens to serve him a well-prepared meal, he may say, "She knows I appreciated it. I ate it, didn't I? I don't *have* to tell her I enjoyed it."

The general difficulty with this type of reasoning is that if a wife says nothing about a husband's work in and around the house, he is not certain whether she appreciates his work or not. Likewise, a husband may eat meals—not because they are tasty and enjoyable—but because it is "polite" or because he is hungry. Hence, a wife is not sure whether her husband is truly happy with a meal simply because he partakes of it. He might go so far, of course, as to compliment her on a dinner and not be sincere, but this is a matter calling for a consideration of openness, truthfulness, and integrity between spouses (a subject we treated in Chapter 1).

The need for complimenting one's spouse, however, must not be overlooked, since this is important not only for building up faltering egos and self-images but for encouraging a sense of responsibility. Otherwise, the desire and motivation for continuing to share the burdens of life with one's partner in marriage slip away and turn into monotonous boredom and drudgery.

One wife said: "He never seems to appreciate anything I do around our home. Either he says nothing or he criticizes. And when he doesn't make any comment, I feel he just doesn't want to criticize me openly. Lately he has been the one caring for the baby and the house more than I. And though he's silent about the way I care for our child and the house, I'm sure he is critical."

Her husband's answer to all this was that he had been trying to relieve her of much of the routine work at home. And, moreover, when his father deserted his mother some years before, he had learned to care for the younger children and maintain the house. He was not, however, critical of his wife.

What had happened to this couple was that the husband had failed to compliment his wife from time to time for her care of the home and child. He had also failed to recognize some of the images he had carried into married life. These images had led him, unknowingly, to assume duties that were within the province of his wife's responsibilities. Since she had few obligations outside the home and was in good physical and emotional health, his doing these tasks puzzled and irritated her.

The routine tasks of life, then, as well as the special ones, should be recognized as matters deserving praise and gratitude. The degree of appreciation expressed should, of course, be in harmony with the nature of the task performed. Projects of an ordinary, everyday type will receive a simple but honest "thank you"; special tasks requiring extra effort and skill will be given proportionately more praise and appreciation.

The Irresponsible Mate

Mates who do not carry their share of the obligations may be encouraged to do so by praising them for their work, eliminating personal criticism, and showing faith and trust in them as they seek to take on increasing responsibility.

It is threatening for a wife, however, to see an irresponsible husband suddenly change his style of living and become ever more capable of assuming his share of the marital duties. She may become extremely uncomfortable because the change in his attitude implies the need for a corresponding change in hers. That is, if he is to become responsible for certain tasks, his wife must be willing to surrender them, perhaps gradually, even though she may be skillful and efficient at them herself. Initially, he may not fulfil his responsibilities as effectively as she did. But if he is to gain experience and self-confidence (many times through trial and error), she must be willing to stand aside, give up the tasks, and control her feelings of anxiety and concern. This may be especially difficult in such matters as paying bills, balancing the budget, caring for cars, or maintaining the house. Harry and Kay were faced with just this type of situation.

Harry had been drinking for a number of years. Though he was not an alcoholic (to the extent of missing work or losing his job), he nevertheless did spend considerable time and money drinking. All the duties he previously performed became her responsibility. In time, he began to improve and show an interest in resuming some of the household duties. Feelings of insecurity and even anger disturbed Kay with this development, and it was necessary to help her gain insight into her own emotional dynamics, while simultaneously giving her support and assurance for the risk-experience she was undergoing.

Wives of alcoholics frequently face this type of situation. The husband is incapable of handling his responsibilities, and the wife is forced to include them in her duties, which may involve many other operations ranging from child rearing to outside employment. In a therapeutic program for her husband, however, she must demonstrate her faith in him, treating him like an adult, not like a child who is incapable of assuming responsibility. This will involve yielding to him those duties that are typically the responsibilities of males in our society. She will be concerned, of course, about the possible cost to the family if such an "experiment" fails and disorganization once again strikes the family operations. It would be better, some wives in such circumstances tend to feel, to continue their program rather than risk a possible family upheaval. Yet this is precisely what must *not* be done, or the spouse will never develop a sense of responsibility—something that is needed for his own feeling of self-respect and for the general welfare of the family. Kessel and Walton have described the apprehension of such wives:

> The competent wife who has become used to making all the decisions and to handling the finances of the family is not always ready to surrender these responsibilities to her spouse though he is eager to resume them. Justifiably she fears that, if he relapses, then once again he will plunge them all into chaos from which they were slowly and painfully rescued by her own exertions and resourcefulness.[3]

If a wife is willing through all the anxiety and experimentation to love, to see things done inexpertly at the first but to go on encouraging her husband, he will probably handle his renewed responsibilities as efficiently as she did. In any case, he will be functioning as a responsible male and will contribute more than if he had continued in his previous irresponsible role.

[3]*Alcoholism*, p. 157.

Unity of Effort in a Marriage

They were seriously considering divorce proceedings. As a matter of fact, he had already contacted a lawyer, but he was willing "to make one more try at working things out." They had married somewhat later in life than most couples, and each had developed his own interests and programs within a framework of relatively complete self-sufficiency. She retained her job, made a feeble attempt to fit into her husband's schedule, but finding little room in it, settled back into her own way of living, as he had into his. After several years of marriage, during which the husband did little to provide direction for either of them in regard to vocational or family planning (though she had started building a bank account to help pay some of the expenses connected with the care of a child in the event he should consent to one), she decided one night to leave a note for him, indicating her discouragement and frustration over their marital situation. It was at this point that they came for professional help.

In time, it became obvious that this wife was trying to manipulate her husband into fulfilling some of her very normal desires. But he was so accustomed to living independently that he was largely impervious to her needs. In any case, he was not about to surrender the management of his life to her. The need was for him to give direction and leadership to the marriage and for her to recognize that she should not attempt to manipulate him. Each needed to help the other achieve a satisfying life. Through the process of counseling, both eventually acknowledged what they had to do to reach this goal.

The ultimate aim, of course, should be to create a marriage of two responsible partners, each complementing the other, so that unity characterizes the marriage. This is not to suggest that there should be no administrative head of the family. As we have seen, studies show that human organizations, whether they comprise two persons or thousands, must have one individual leading them if serious conflict and frustration are to be avoided. James Mooney makes this point when he writes of the necessity for leadership and unity even when only two people are involved in a common task:

> Take two men who combine their efforts to lift and move a stone that is too heavy to be moved by one. . . . To begin with, the two lifters must lift in unison. . . . Likewise one of these two must give the signal "heave ho!" or its equivalent, to the other, thus illustrating the principle of *leadership*.[4]

A dictatorship need not result from this kind of arrangement. In the case of a husband and wife, mutual love should provide an atmosphere that permits each to fulfil his functions and develop his individual identity within a unified structure under the general direction of the husband. Bailey has written that

> man's "superiority," like [the woman's] "subjection," is also rooted in the will of God, and is attested by his possessing by nature faculties for organization, direction, and government which normally surpass hers. . . . The husband's rule and the wife's subjection must both be in love. As Christians they have already submitted to one another "in the fear of Christ," in whom sexual distinction possesses no ultimate meaning; . . . as husband, however, the man is the "head" of his wife, and as wife, the woman is "in subjection" to her husband.[5]

The two primary advantages of direction and unity of this kind within the family are efficiency and lowered frustration levels. Without unity, the efficient allocation of resources is difficult, since there is seldom enough to meet all the wishes and aspirations of the human personality, with its sometimes exceedingly high and unrealistic goals.

[4]In *Papers on the Science of Administration* (ed. L. Gulick and L. Urwick), p. 91.

[5]*The Mystery of Love and Marriage*, pp. 132f.

Whatever money, time, and energy are available must be distributed as fairly as possible. But there may be real disagreement over what is "fair." Hence the need for someone to make the final decision, especially if a frustrating impasse should develop. The results of final decisions, however, should minimize frustration, strengthen the family, foster the planning process, and assist in attaining both family and individual goals in an organized fashion.

Long-range and short-range planning should, of course, be carried out to as great a degree as possible in all areas of life. The responsibility for this rests with the husband. Wives frequently complain that husbands fail to do either long-range or short-range planning. "Living like this," a wife will say, "not knowing from one minute to the next what we will be doing or where we will be going is making a nervous wreck out of me." One wife, who was understandably irritated, remarked:

"My husband will be lying on the couch in the living room watching television late on a Saturday morning. Without warning he will get up and announce, 'I think I'd like to go to the zoo today. Get the kids together and let's go.' I'm thrown into a panic because he is so inconsiderate. He doesn't seem to realize that most of the time the children have to be washed, clothed, and fed before we go, or they will look unkempt and be unmanageable if they're hungry. But he doesn't seem to take all the factors into consideration when he wants to do something. If only he would do a little planning and give me some time to make arrangements and get things in order."

In other words, there is a need for husbands to think ahead, to consider the many tasks involved in a family project, and to do both short- and long-range planning, just as they undoubtedly do in the professional and business world.

The Impatient Wife

Wives often present a somewhat different type of problem to their husbands. A husband may be occupied with an undertaking of some kind—anything from reading the paper to cleaning the garage. His wife may ignore the fact that most people in the midst of a project, whatever its nature, would like to complete it if it only requires a short period of time. The prevailing sentiment among many wives is, if a husband refuses to drop what he is doing and *immediately* begin work on her request, to do it herself rather than wait around for him to get to it. One wife admitted that she had treated her husband this way many times. Eventually she recognized her need to make a request several minutes before it actually had to be carried out, rather than waiting until the last minute and then being impatient because he failed to react instantly.

Psychologically, there is the fear of manipulation in such a situation. Each spouse values his independence. And one way for him to preserve his independent feeling and status is to insist on the right to carry out the spouse's wish when it can be fitted into his schedule. He wants to retain the right to decide *when* a thing will be done, even though he has not decided *what* is to be done.

A free and independent person will usually try to reserve for himself the right to decide as many of these matters as he can. A spouse, therefore, may ask his mate to do a certain job, but the mate has the right to decide when and how that will be done, thus helping him hold on to his dignity as a person with a measure of independence and self-determination.

Employment and Home Responsibilities

A special area needing careful consideration is that involving the choice of vocational goals and their relationship to household duties. In the past, it was largely the husband who was concerned with the choice of a vocation. But increasingly women are taking positions in the business world and the professions. Sometimes it is a financial or emotional factor that forces a woman into outside employment. A wife and mother may find that when her children have grown up and left home, she is left with very few responsibilities around the house, most of which may be completed in a few hours a day. With the prospect of 25 to 30 years of life before her, she may well desire to use her remaining available time and energy in the most stimulating, profitable, and fulfilling way.

It may be the search for an identity complementing that of wife and mother that motivates her to seek employment. Teaching, social work, or contributing a skill to the business world could well turn out to be her new interest and desire. Any proposed change in a wife's activities, however, may imply a new pattern of living. If there is love, understanding, and willingness to adapt, husbands and wives will be able to review their responsibilities and divide them in accord with their individual needs.

Interdependence

Much of what we have said in this chapter points to the complementarity and interdependence of husbands and wives. Of course, there is no perfect formula for the relationship of all husbands and wives. But this much can be said: just as no nation or business firm wishes to be completely dependent on another, but seeks a relative degree of independence, this principle is of the essence of the marriage relationship too.

Freedom, dignity, and a responsible independence are usually desired by everyone. Yet no one is completely independent or self-sufficient. Only as a realistic *inter*-dependence is maintained can couples, nations, businesses, and individuals achieve their unique goals. For a person who wishes to "go it alone," the time soon comes when cooperation from others disappears, isolation develops, and existence itself becomes a problem. In other words, interdependence is a fact of life. It, therefore, becomes a matter for husbands and wives of working out complementary roles that are mutually and responsibly fulfilling, recognizing that the perfect program in an imperfect world is never attainable.

Summary

1. Whenever two persons embark upon a joint venture like marriage, both must be willing to assume a degree of responsibility if the venture is to be successful. Few joint undertakings can succeed with only one of the parties shouldering responsibility.

2. The extent to which one is willing to assume marital responsibility may be influenced largely by the parental expectation-images that he developed prior to marriage. Such images should be thoroughly discussed by couples seeking to develop satisfactory marital relationships.

3. Not only special but routine achievements by a spouse should be praised, when this can be done sincerely and appropriately, since this enhances self-esteem and motivates the individual to continue carrying his responsibilities as part of the joint marital enterprise.

4. When a formerly irresponsible mate begins to assume duties within the marital framework, the spouse who previously carried such duties will probably feel reluctant to surrender them, since the newly motivated mate may not do them as efficiently. But such feelings of reluctance and anxiety must not hinder the transfer of these duties, or a sharing of responsibilities will be difficult to achieve.

5. One important goal is to provide the marriage with a unified framework having two responsible and co-

operating partners, so that personal and marital objectives will be achieved efficiently.

6. In today's world, with its many opportunities for employment and increased longevity, discussions of planned allocations of time, energy, and resources must be conducted if a productive interdependence and fair division of labor are to result for both husbands and wives.

7. Developing an Identity

Meaning of Identity

There is considerable discussion today by both men and women about finding or creating a personal identity. In past generations, most individuals concerned themselves with acquiring a quality education so they could meet the goals of self and family preservation. But today the concerns of life extend beyond such goals to the achievement of identity and its related objectives of meaning and self-fulfilment.

The term "identity" refers to a consistent set of character traits or images regarding the self in relation to other persons. According to Erik Erikson, "it connotes both a persistent sameness within oneself (selfsameness) and a persistent sharing of some kind of essential character with others."[1] This implies that the concepts one forms about himself must always incorporate ideas of his relationships with others, what others conceive him to be, and what images they have of him. In the words of James Peterson, "to finally know oneself as a unique individual, to accept that self as worthy, and then to share that worthy uniqueness with others, is all part of the task of discovering and developing one's identity."[2]

Implicit in speaking of "developing or attaining an identity" is the thought of uniqueness and self-fulfilment.

[1] "Identity and the Life Cycle," *Psychological Issues,* I, No. 1, 102.
[2] *Married Love in the Middle Years,* pp. 60f.

No one likes to believe he is identical to another personality. Yet if he sees little significant difference between his functions and those of other individuals, he experiences a role diffusion and a sense of depersonalization. He begins to ask who he really is, since he seems to be like so many other persons. From the depths of his being he wants to feel that he is a *person* with a unique destiny. But his life experiences, his self-concepts, and the persons who are important to him may not create in him a sense of his uniqueness and significance. So he begins a personal quest for attaining an identity that includes the goals of uniqueness, significance, and self-fulfilment.

Sexual Roles in the Home

One of the most critical factors in identity formation is that of sexual differentiation and sexual identity. Inevitably, if one cannot feel like a member of his own sex, and sufficiently distinct from the opposite sex, frustration and insecurity will result. Each culture appears to have its own methods and techniques for inducting its members into their appropriate sex roles so that frustration is kept within tolerable limits, but the principle of differentiation is for all practical purposes universal. Clothing, social rituals, religious ceremonies, permanent identifying marks, hair and face coloring, heterosexual patterns of conduct, and assignment of work all contribute to the personality formation of males and females.

Many of the distinguishing criteria are derived from our biological make-up. For instance, because of their physical strength, men are more involved in law enforcement and heavy physical labor, whereas women are concerned with the care of children and the lighter domestic duties of cooking and maintaining the home. However, because of technological advancements in recent years, it is much easier for women to serve in areas once reserved for men. It is also possible for men, with the aid of household devices such as dishwashers, vacuum cleaners, ready-to-eat dinners, and child-care centers, to carry out many of the responsibilities that were once the exclusive province of women. This sets the stage for sex-role confusion and anxiety over sexual and personal identity. Some scholars argue that the drive for establishing a sexual identity is one of the reasons for the high rate of illegitimate births: the man seeks to prove his masculinity through aggressive sexual acts and the woman her femininity by bearing children. In any case, the need for a clear sexual identity is basic to healthy personality formation and highly important for satisfactory adjustment and functioning in our society.

Since Christian principles and contemporary social mores call for the proper differentiation of the sexes, it is well for couples to work out their sexual task roles within the home in the early years of marriage. The husband will, in general, provide in a material way for the family (I Tim. 5:8) and give it a sense of unity (Eph. 5:23). The wife will feel the primary responsibility for the care of the home and the children (Titus 2:4, 5). A couple should also analyze their family backgrounds in order to identify the practices they wish to continue and those which appear inappropriate for them. A check against the norms of society (through reading, through counseling, etc.) regarding the sex roles of husbands and wives will help give them some notion of the ways that may be best for them, particularly since their roles should be compatible with social customs, insofar as these do not conflict with biblical values and standards.

If there are children, fathers and mothers must be adequate sexual models. This makes the proper distribution of tasks and responsibilities in the home all the more important. Anyone familiar with case histories of children with confused sex roles recognizes the crucial influence of parental example. Serious attention should be given, therefore, to the kinds of interpersonal behavior patterns established by parents.

Despite the fact that mothers may be employed outside the home in what is known as a "man's world," they can nevertheless make a special effort to conduct themselves in definitely feminine ways, so that daughters will develop healthy identifications with them and sons will relate to them in an appropriate and nonconfusing fashion. Fathers may help by giving preference to tasks requiring greater physical strength (painting the exterior of a house, building fences, and the like). If fathers, also, exercise authority appropriately, leading the family with wisdom and fairness, this should further help family members make healthy and positive sexual identifications.

Ackerman has well stressed the need for the family unit to support the identity formation of its individual members. He says:

> The identity of the individual requires support from family identity. . . . The relations of individual and family are characterized by a delicate interplay of parallel processes of emotional joining and separation. Out of the basic union come individuation and new growth, but each stage of individuation in turn calls for the discovery of new levels of sharing and union.[3]

Closely tied into one's sexual identity is his attitude toward his physical body. Those who work in the field of mental health have long recognized the close relationship of healthy sex attitudes and the acceptance of one's own sex and body image. Colby states that

> what [the patient] thinks of his body as a source of pleasure or discomfort and how he perceives reality in terms of his body concept are integral to all of his ideas and imagery. Body size or shape, beauty or ugliness, wholeness or handicap, and skill or clumsiness also may represent significant determinants in psychological processes.[4]

[3] *Treating the Troubled Family*, p. 60.
[4] *A Primer for Psychotherapists*, p. 10.

Some women, for instance, do not accept the female figure. They say that they see nothing beautiful about a woman's body, and they find themselves negative toward its anatomical and physiological structure. To feel this way cannot help influencing one's self-concept. Height, weight, texture of hair, complexion, birthmarks, irregularities or deformities, and other physical factors all contribute to the attitude one holds about his sexual and personal identity. Unhealthy or unrealistic concepts regarding one's sex and sexual role, therefore, should be corrected not only for his own personal well-being but also for the sake of any children who may be consciously or unconsciously identifying with him.

Vocational Pursuits

The choices a person makes in life contribute to the identity he is forming. Some of these are more important than others; surely one of the most important is selection of a career. The satisfaction a person derives from his vocation, however, depends largely on the recognition that persons he thinks significant provide him. A man may be involved in work that is difficult, monotonous, and lacking in social status, but if he gains reinforcement and appreciation from his family or other important persons, he will usually find sufficient meaning in his labors to satisfy him. Likewise, a woman may be simultaneously engaged as a housewife and teacher, secretary, or nurse and feel emotionally fulfilled as a person, particularly if her husband, the family, and others praise and respect her. On the other hand, if the significant persons in one's life do not reveal a positive attitude toward the career program being followed, a sense of frustration and inadequacy is frequently the outcome. This was the case of John and Mary.

John had worked for several years in his profession with relative success and praise from his wife. Things changed, however, and before long Mary grew irritable over the many social engagements and professional contacts that required her cooperation and presence. Eventually, she found herself just "too tired" to accompany her husband on his evenings out. In time, professional acquaintances and friends began to wonder why John and Mary were seldom seen together. This affected John's work so that he became anxious over the criticism directed at him, with the result that ulcers and physically related symptoms developed, forcing him to change his profession.

A different type of situation was that of Joyce and Tom. Joyce, with her husband's encouragement, sought a new career as part of her self-fulfilment.

Joyce and Tom had been married for 15 years and had several children. Tom's lack of higher education and social skills combined with a preference for working around the house made it possible for Joyce to consider a career in art. She made arrangements to take lessons in oil painting in order to develop the natural artistic talents which were already much in evidence. Eventually, some of her paintings sold, bringing to the family some additional income. The important thing for Joyce was that the work brought fulfilment and contributed to the establishment of an identity which she had sought all her life—to be not only a wife and mother, but also an artist. She and her husband were comparatively happy with the arrangement and each achieved a satisfying identity, which capitalized on their specifically individual aptitudes, interests, and abilities.

The opportunity for wives to work outside the home keeps increasing. Assuming that there is no intention of avoiding a family or depriving an existing family of proper care, and that a satisfactory arrangement can be worked out with the husband, there is no reason why wives should not seek employment. An identity involving specialized vocational pursuits is certainly possible for many women. With smaller families, increased longevity, and reduced responsibilities in the home, it is realistic to think in terms of employment for both the husband and wife, insofar as they agree upon their programs and mutual satisfactions are attainable. In the final analysis, however, vocation for both Christian husbands and wives should be in harmony with the will of God.

Barth has said in regard to this subject that the vocation of man is to be understood as a decree of God and as man's answer to the divine calling.[5]

Values and Identity Formation

Many values enter into the decision-making process affecting the establishment of identities for husbands and wives. All of these should be seen in proper perspective. For example, one person may want great freedom in terms of time to develop an artistic or musical skill. Another may be so committed to social or religious pursuits that only a thoroughly sympathetic spouse would be willing to cooperate with him in his heavy schedule of activities. Of course, values exist in persons in a constantly changing fashion, so that first one value and then another is most important. Also, various combinations of primary values, rather than a single value, may influence the choice of one's activities.

> In most individuals there exists a *hierarchical* order as far as their values are concerned, whether they know it or not. . . . They want an all-around fulfillment, and they can temporarily switch from emphasizing one particular value to any of the others. . . . That is to say, they may at one time want more than anything to accomplish something worthwhile, then they want more than anything to have a period of pleasure, of vacation, of relaxation, then may come a period in which they are concerned with their duties to their family and their

[5]*Church Dogmatics*, III/4, 634.

friends, then they may want to meditate and concentrate on problems of their own inner peace of mind.[6]

Because an individual's value hierarchy is constantly shifting, there must be sufficient awareness and openness to communicate with one's mate so that crucial choices can be made.

A woman at one point in her life may feel that equality of opportunity for developing intellectual or job skills is a less important value than commitment to her children. She may also limit her freedom of choice because there is greater meaning and significance in life if she remains at home rather than working in the business world. After the children have entered school or left home, however, her value hierarchy may become rearranged so that what was originally subordinate becomes primary. The need for open communication between marital partners is obvious from the fact that the husband's value system may not change at precisely the same moment as his wife's. If conflict over planning their future activities is to be avoided, she must be willing to discuss her aspirations with her husband, even as he should discuss his aspirations with her as his value system changes. In this way, adjustments can be made with minimal emotional upheaval between them.

Let us now look at some of the values that influence our behavior greatly and what they imply for attaining a personal identity.

a) *Freedom of Choice.* Since it is the person himself who knows most intimately his desires, interests, and aspirations, no one else should make the choices that determine his identity. Others may assist him in evaluating his assets and liabilities, but only *he* is aware of the depth of his concern for certain life goals. He must be sufficiently free so that various realistic options or alternatives are available to him for the process of identity formation. This is not a total or absolute freedom; anarchy would be the only

[6]Charlotte Buhler, *Values in Psychotherapy*, p. 166.

possible result if everyone had unlimited freedom without any restraints whatever. But freedom of choice recognizes the right of the individual to select one plan as opposed to another *within a context of responsibility.* For, as Victor Frankl says, "being human is being responsible because it is being free."[7]

In exercising its freedom, the human spirit opens the door to creativity as well as integrity and identity. Only as the individual lives and works in a climate of freedom will he tend to cultivate his creative abilities, develop a sense of responsibility, choose to be open, and form an identity consonant with his inner potentialities. Admittedly, much of man's life in the past has been determined by forces largely out of his control. But because of man's freedom to choose, he has increased his knowledge so that today he is capable of regulating his life and environment to a greater degree than ever before (for example, he has the ability to control his health and the size of his family, to communicate with other sections of the world almost instantly, and to transport himself quickly and inexpensively to points of great distance); thus, he has created for himself conditions which can foster his maximum personal growth.

b) *Commitment.* This refers to giving one's total being to another person or the pursuit of some object to the exclusion of all others. Marriage is "the ideal type of formal commitment to a tie of common identity,"[8] and is also important for developing the individual identities of a husband and wife. As long as this value is strong within a marriage, there is great possibility for a couple to become the persons they are potentially in both an individual and collective way. Without it, suspicion, anxiety, hostility, jealousy, and bitterness usually result, with accompanying emotional disturbance and severe interruption of one's program of identity building.

[7] *The Doctor and the Soul,* p. 76.

[8] N. N. Foote and L. S. Cottrell, Jr., *Identity and Interpersonal Competence,* p. 172.

Commitment may ultimately be directed toward God and can become the means for helping an individual attain the unique identity for which he is intended. Commitment in this sense is brought about through faith in Jesus Christ as Lord and Savior. It may contribute significantly to the formation of one's secular identity, but it is more concerned with the individual's identity as a person, with eternal worth, and with the salvation of his soul, that is, with his spiritual identity and destiny.

c) *Dignity of the Individual.* The value of the human person is ultimately derived from the worth that God Himself has placed upon him. The very fact that God gave His Son to redeem (or purchase) eternal life for man, places supreme value upon each individual. If the Creator so values men, then all who believe and follow Him will likewise see worth in man and therefore hold him in respect. The preciousness of human life and the worth of every individual calls for proper and humane treatment of all persons. Husbands must respect their wives as those who have personal rights under God, treating them courteously, kindly, and gently. Wives should seek to understand and respect their husbands, who also have rights, needs, and feelings.

Children, however young they may be, should be given fair and gentle treatment as persons, too. The "Battered Child Syndrome"—the physical mistreatment of infants and very young children—is a sharp violation of the dignity of the human person. All persons, whatever their age, sex, ethnic background, or religious convictions, deserve respect and humane care and treatment because God has invested them with personal worth, value, and dignity.

This sense of worth and respect assists in releasing original and creative forces in each person and makes it possible for them to seek and ultimately realize their true identity. Without such respect, the search for identity would be lost in a milieu of cruelty, selfishness, and lack of respect for human life and individual rights.

d) *Equality.* Although people are not equal in intelligence, social status, or physical attributes, the Christian's attitude should be one of interacting with others as those who, before God, *are* equal with him as members of the human race. Again, the derivation of this value has its ground and existence in God Himself. He has instructed Christians to treat others as equals and not to "have respect to persons" (James 2:9). Personhood, like salvation, is a gift from God and cannot be earned. Implicit in an attitude of equality toward all men is that each person should have equality of opportunity so that he may develop himself as fully as possible. Even in a society in which equality of opportunity appears to be lacking, it is incumbent on all Christians to help improve social conditions so that there is a desire to seek an approximation of the ideal as much as possible.

Equality of opportunity in respect to identity formation, therefore, should be available to everyone. That is, there should be opportunity to become a person whose unique qualities have been developed and maximized, thereby leading to a sense of self-fulfilment. This, of course, should be one of the general goals of marriage, so that as a social institution it contributes to forming an identity for the husband and for the wife as separate persons in their own right.

The importance of equality of opportunity for identity attainment for both husbands and wives cannot be stressed too greatly. Yet, as Dicks has warned, the identities sought by men and women must include the typical behaviors for males and females respectively. That is, men must be linked to operations that lead toward economic security and social-occupational status for the family, and women to the cherishing, nourishing, and maternal functions. "Few marriages," he states, "can endure when these primary biological tasks are completely denied, or even if some of the secondary roles deriving from them are too flagrantly reversed."[9]

Ultimate Identity

In the final nature of things, a man's destiny—a man's identity, in the complete sense of the term—is bound up with God and His Son Jesus Christ. And just as there was significance and purpose and uniqueness in His life, this can also be made possible for those who follow Him.

> The gospel affirms that the chasm between God and man is traversed in the person of Jesus Christ. . . . Here, as Calvin insisted, knowledge of God and man's knowledge of himself are reconciled. Man claims his own humanity by the self-transcending act of identifying himself with Christ in faith. . . . Man's implicit identity is made explicit in Christ.[10]

For the one who finds his identity completed in Christ there will be purpose, pattern, and meaning. It may well include maximal self-realization, so that most or all of his potentialities are used for the glory of God. Or it may require the surrender of certain skills and abilities more than others. This is especially true for individuals who are gifted in many areas. But where there is love, openness, integrity, and a sincere desire to work out compatible programs for identity attainment, making choices for identity formation is much easier. And if all of life comes under the guidance and direction of God Himself, those who would know and find their true identity should undoubtedly come to realize it.

---

[9]*Marital Tensions*, p. 33.

[10]C. R. Stinnette, Jr., "Reflection and Transformation: Knowing and Change in Psychotherapy and in Religious Faith," in *The Dialogue Between Theology and Psychology* (ed. Peter Homans), pp. 90f.

Summary

1. Every person wants to feel that life has meaning for him and that he has a uniqueness that distinguishes him from other persons. The set of traits and images that an individual develops contributes to the establishment of a uniqueness known as his identity.

2. A healthy and meaningful identity depends to a great extent on the adequate development of one's sexual role in relation to one's spouse as well as to all persons of significance.

3. Vocational pursuits are integral to one's identity. Husbands and wives, therefore, need to consider each others' skills, needs, and aptitudes in selecting careers and life goals. Some women may seek to complete their identity through work outside the home and others may not. In any case, the primary biological tasks (e.g., sexual intercourse and conceiving children) and the secondary roles deriving from these tasks (for example, the man's responsibility for providing economic security and the woman's for cherishing and performing maternal functions) should not be neglected, since few marriages can survive when these tasks are completely denied.

4. Many values enter into the decisions determining our identity. Freedom of choice, commitment, dignity of the individual, and equality of opportunity are examples.

5. Ultimate identity involves the fulfilment of God-given purposes. A recognition of this enables one to discover his true and complete identity, which is to be found only by faith in God and His Son Jesus Christ.

8. The Sexual Factor

There are many strange and unfounded concepts held by both men and women about the sex relationship. These are deeply imbedded in thought processes and behavior patterns early in life, because they permeate our culture in books, laws, folklore, community mores, and parental value systems. Without testing these concepts biblically or scientifically, they are passed along from generation to generation as infallible guides to personal conduct.

As those committed to the search for and communication of truth, we are obliged to correct misconceptions and distorted ideas. We must also be willing to accept the fact that truth tends to filter very gradually into thoughts and personality patterns. This is as true for the sexual dimension of personality as it is for all others. If married couples will recognize that truth is important but often takes root in personality slowly, the necessary patience and understanding will no doubt be available for overcoming unhealthy sex concepts and for developing satisfactory sexual relationships.

The Physical Relationship

It is important for the reader to differentiate between the terms *sex* and *sexuality* as used in theological and psychological literature. "Sex" usually refers to the physical dimension of the marriage relationship, including education in the physiological functioning of the genital organs, purposes of the sex relationship, and the physical expression of love in the preparation for and process of intercourse. "Sexuality" involves all of the relationships, including that of sex, which occur between man as truly masculine and woman as truly feminine. Since the previous chapters have dealt with many of the aspects of sexuality, this chapter will focus primarily on the physical relationship that we call sex.

Two questions that numerous couples have asked about the sex relationship are: "Should love be limited primarily to words and sexual intercourse reserved for the begetting of children?" and "Can the body be a healthy medium for expressing affection for one's mate without procreation necessarily being the sole reason for the relationship?" In seeking to answer these questions, negative concepts have been offered regarding the nature, function, and purpose of the body as well as of sexual intercourse itself. Increasingly, however, Christian leaders are stressing that the body is a means for good, and that sexual intercourse has two very positive and primary purposes: the expression of love between husbands and wives and the propagation of children.

This implies that the physical relationship is not to be confined to the begetting of children, but that there is a spiritual purpose served when husbands and wives engage in sexual intercourse, whether or not children are intended. To think otherwise would preclude the sexual relationship between husband and wife during such periods as pregnancy (although physicians may suggest abstinence during the last few weeks or months), the period following childbirth prior to the resumption of ovulation, after a hysterectomy (removal of the uterus) or after the menopause (which may occur as early as the middle thirties for some women). Instead, there should be a continuous mutuality of love that is communicated through the sex relationship. This, in turn, symbolizes the mystery of the unity of husband and wife as ordained by God.

One of the unfortunate misconceptions held by many

121

husbands and wives in the past is that the body and its activities are essentially sinful. The Christian church itself has at times contributed to this by misinterpreting the conflict between the scriptural concepts of "flesh" and "spirit," implying that the human body and the "spirit" are at cross-purposes. Though this interpretation has been repeatedly pronounced as erroneous, people still tend to equate the physical body with the term "flesh."

> The Christian cannot accept the pagan notion that body (flesh) and matter are evil while mind and things of the spirit alone are good. . . . The battle is not against flesh but against sin—so that the reborn man may glorify God in body as well as spirit (Rom. 6:12, 13). . . . In Christian thinking the body is neither despised nor idolized (as among the heathen), but it is held to be holy, consecrated to God as His temple (I Cor. 6:15, 19, 20).[1]

Moreover, St. Paul instructs husbands and wives *not* to defraud one another of the sex relationship. As Phillips translates it in his *Letters to Young Churches:*

> The husband should give his wife what is due to her as his wife, and the wife should be as fair to her husband. The wife has no longer full rights over her own person, but shares them with her husband. In the same way the husband shares his personal rights with his wife. Do not cheat each other of normal sexual intercourse, unless of course you both decide to abstain temporarily to make special opportunity for fasting and prayer. But afterwards you should resume relations as before . . . (I Cor. 7:3-5).

According to the principle of Scripture, then, the sexual function of the body must not be viewed as sinful or evil but rather as good and necessary for healthy Christian marriage.

A parallel concern of many couples involves the right-ness of physical love play and caressing prior to the sexual

[1] Oscar Feucht (ed.), *Sex and the Church,* p. 103.

122

act. This becomes immaterial, however, if the physical attention is motivated by true love of the husband for his wife, or a wife for her husband, since the body and spirit are given over to one of the divine purposes in marriage, namely, the expression of love. The *intention* of a couple, of course, should be that of completing their love with the act of sex relations, but if intercourse is not advisable, this should not preclude the various forms of physical affection. Insofar as the affection given by spouses to each other is motivated by a desire to love unselfishly, it is of an *agape* or all-giving nature, and, according to Bailey, is an inclusive love that permeates all other types of love, imbuing them with a love of divine origin. He states that *agape*—unselfish love—denotes:

> . . . not only the distinctive Christian love, but also the altruistic, self-giving principle inherent in all true love—the activity of the will whereby *eros* is governed and *philia* enriched, and the good of the beloved and of the *henosis* is placed first . . . *agape* pervades the relation as a whole.[2]

Husbands and wives, therefore, should belong to each other and enjoy each other fully, as the Book of Proverbs suggests: ". . . rejoice with the wife of thy youth . . . let her breasts satisfy thee at all times; and be thou ravished always with her love" (5:18-19).

The Conscientious Male

Men inculcated with Christian values and attitudes by their parents usually have great respect for womanhood. They wish to protect the rights of their wives as persons and not to be unfair or cruel in any way. Yet it is possible for a man to become overly tolerant toward his wife in the sex relationship to the extent of denying his own masculinity. He may be reluctant to initiate love play or the act of intercourse because he fears violating his wife's wishes

[2]*The Mystery of Love and Marriage,* p. 28.

or sensitivities. Moreover, he may have been taught to "bring his body under subjection" and never to give the impression that his sex impulses are strong and powerful. The problem with this is that he is a man and she is a woman, each with a different dynamic balance of psychological and physiological forces.

Studies by Masters and Johnson[3] have shown that men, in contrast to women, are more easily stimulated by many of the words and pictures in our sex-conscious society. Billboards, magazines, television, radio, and a host of other media constantly employ advertising techniques that tend to exploit sex. Though most women are not consciously aroused by many of these environmental stimuli, men unquestionably are. This is one of the reasons why men appear to be more sexually aggressive and to have less control.

It is not uncommon, however, to find extremely unhealthy and repressive controls of the sexual impulse on the part of overly gentle and conscientious husbands. Along with this condition, there is usually a lack of sexual aggressiveness in the act of sexual intercourse itself. An example of this is found in the case of Don and Betty.

Don's age and physical stature seemed to indicate that he was a very normal and virile male. Yet when he discussed the matter of sex relations, he said, "It's not necessary for me. I can get along with it, or I can get along without it." Several sessions later, however, he became quite angry about their situation and blurted out: "Any woman who has sex relations only once every four or five weeks with her husband just doesn't understand men!"

Don's masculine self finally began to assert itself, and he became extremely angry about the sexual deprivation he had experienced. The reason for his excessive sexual

[3]See their volume *Human Sexual Response.*

control and lack of aggressiveness was a belief that the Christian husband should not insist on sex relations, for this would not be "proper." Thus, he was passive, controlled, and undemanding, which was contrary to his true masculine nature. When this was brought out in Don and Betty's therapy program, it was used as a basis for modifying and improving their sexual pattern.

A similar case involved a husband who was overly careful about expressing his desire for sexual intercourse and found his wife dissatisfied with his unusually well-controlled sexual drive.

Harold and Dorothy had been married for two years and had enjoyed their married life together immensely until her attitude changed toward the sex relationship. Apparently, neither of them had initiated the sex relationship during the first two years of marriage, but had devised a system of "signals" that was so delicately balanced that neither perceived the other as the initiator. Contributing to all this was Harold's view that men should be gentle and not insist upon sex relations.

Dorothy, however, tired of sharing equally in initiating sex relations and began to yearn for Harold to be "all male" and the aggressor in the relationship. This, she felt, would be far more thrilling and exciting for her. So she became passive, waiting for him to make the first move. He was confused over this development because their system of "signals" was now no longer working. He was reluctant to impose sex relations upon her, since he felt that "that would not be Christian," and she refused to tell him that the previous signaling arrangement was no longer operative.

What Dorothy wanted was for Harold's masculine nature to drive him toward her. Her desire was to feel physically wanted, but without telling him so. The changing of the rules, however, the lack of self-disclosure, and the repression of Harold's masculine desires placed a great strain on their marriage. She failed to understand his rigid system of values in regard to the sex relationship, he failed to be himself, and they both failed to disclose their true feelings to each other. As a result, the very existence of the marriage hung in the balance for a time. When Harold was told that his wife actually hoped for his insistence on sex relations, he replied, "Really? I never thought she felt that way!" From that point on, their relationship began to show greater openness and subsequent improvement.

This is not to suggest that husbands should be crude or unrefined in this sensitive area of marital life. Wives, nevertheless, do want their husbands to be masculine, even as they themselves wish to be feminine. As the case above illustrates, one of the greatest requirements for solving sexual dilemmas is for openness and honesty between mates. Wives know that most men possess greater physical drive for sexual intercourse than most women. Though a wife may accept a certain degree of sexual passiveness in her husband at the beginning of marriage, she usually becomes dissatisfied with such an arrangement after several years. It is necessary for the husband, therefore, to insist upon sex relations or on an open discussion of the problem *because he is a male.* He must not beg or plead on the grounds that sex relations is a right that goes along with marriage (which it does), but he must by virtue of his masculinity gently but firmly insist on sexual intercourse or initiate a very thorough discussion of their physical relationship, so that steps can be taken to remove whatever emotional or physical blocks may exist.

A good deal of patience will sometimes be required during the discussion of a sex problem, since the time needed for reaching a solution may possibly involve several weeks or months. Anything longer than this should probably receive professional attention.

Frequency of Sex Relations

One of the common disagreements between husbands and wives centers on the frequency of intercourse. Some wives will state that their husbands are far too demanding, bordering on an extreme preoccupation with the sex relationship. "He seems to be interested in nothing but sex since we got married a year ago," a young wife may complain.

Clinical data[4] indicate that most husbands, whether non-Christian or Christian, prefer to have sex relations with approximately the same frequency. The typical husband in his twenties prefers sex relations from three to five times a week (and sometimes more), depending upon the nature of his work and the particular emotional stress that he may undergo from day to day. Men in their thirties prefer sex relations from two to four times a week. And men in their forties usually have a preference for a frequency of one to three times a week. After the age of fifty, there is often a marked decline in sexual desire, with a great many men capable of participating in sexual intercourse on a more or less infrequent basis into their seventies. Factors that affect the ability of men to engage in sex relations include hereditary traits, physical or mental illness, and the general stresses connected with working and living. In the event the male appears to fall short of the norms described, it does not necessarily indicate a lack of masculinity, but perhaps a medical and psychological check-up should be considered.

Since their differences are so marked in the sexual area, husbands and wives should attempt to achieve as complete as possible an understanding of the sexual needs of their spouses. Despite all of the guidance and advice a woman may receive, it is impossible for her truly to understand how a man feels sexually, nor is it possible for him to

[4]A. Kinsey, *et al., Sexual Behavior in the Human Female,* p. 348.

know how she feels. If she is aware of the man's greater need for sexual satisfaction, she may be willing to participate in sex relations even when her own desire may be moderately or extremely low. On the other hand, he should accept the fact that many women reach a point of emotional exhaustion, sometimes due to an extremely difficult day with the children or other stressful experiences, and would prefer to postpone the relationship for a day or so. Openness and honesty, of course, are most important when working out mutually satisfying adjustments in this area.

Spouses should become sensitive, moreover, to the many other factors that tend to influence the desire for, and frequency of, sexual relations. Ignoring the simple rules of hygiene, for example, will create problems.

One very fastidious, middle-class housewife complained about her husband's poor attitude toward cleanliness. "I know he comes from a home background where they only bathed once a week," she stated. "But his job leaves him covered with perspiration, he doesn't use a deodorant, he has dirt under his fingernails, he has bad breath, and because of all these things I find the sex relationship repulsive."

There is little doubt that attention given to *daily* hygiene, especially before retiring, will make the sexual relationship a great deal more inviting and satisfying. One caution should be stressed. If a spouse decides to carry out certain hygienic measures just before retiring, a mate should avoid making negative comments like "I know why you're showering before coming to bed" or "I know why you're brushing your teeth. It's not because you love me, it's just because you want to have sex relations."

A husband or a wife should be understanding and positive toward a mate who wants to improve the sexual relationship. The act of sexual intercourse should always be an experience from which both partners gain satisfaction. It is not a matter of one giving and the other receiving, for this only fragments and quenches love. Both should receive as well as give love.

If a husband showers immediately before retiring, his motives may well include making the anticipated sex experience pleasant for the two of them. If his wife accuses him of being selfish and seeking something from her which she does not wish to give, or from which she will receive no satisfaction, it causes him to feel guilty, because he is pictured as ego-centered, and to feel rejected because she has attacked the motive of love he feels, however intertwined such love may be with his physical desire. Obviously, the need is for understanding and acceptance of any effort directed at improving the sexual relationship, whether the effort comes from the husband or the wife.

The Psychosomatic Factor:
The Interaction of Mind and Body

The term "psychosomatic" refers to the reciprocal or interacting processes of the mind and body. That is, the mind acts on the body and the body on the mind. An example of the mind's affecting the body is the case of an individual who develops ulcers because of a highly anxious and emotional existence (not all ulcers are psychogenic in origin). The reverse situation, in which the body acts upon the mind, is illustrated by the person who is deprived of sufficient sleep for several days and becomes irritable or even hostile—a condition that is quickly relieved once the body obtains its needed rest.

An interaction of mind and body also occurs in connection with the sex act. If a woman's mind is free from distracting thoughts and filled with admiration and love for her husband, she finds the sexual act more physically satisfying. The mind, in this case, influences the responses of the body to the sexual act. The opposite of this is illustrated in the wife whose husband fails to treat her body gently or affectionately in the sexual relationship. Finding no physical satisfaction—though she has read books on marriage that tell of the physical enjoyment she should experience—she soon develops a dislike for sexual intercourse. In the former case, the attitudes of the mind make it possible for the physical experience to be satisfying. In the latter case, the body is deprived of satisfaction (although originally hoped for), and a mental attitude of dislike for the sex relationship results.

Bringing body and mind into a harmonious relationship in the sex experience requires a great deal of genuine effort and cooperation. To do so is a learning experience for each partner. Sometimes considerable time is necessary before the body and mind are sufficiently educated to function together, due to the complicated and complex interaction involved. But both the body and mind must learn. In the final analysis, the aim is to bring the physical and psychological processes under personal and unified control, for only in this way are mind and body brought into an integrated relationship. Once this integration of mind and body has been achieved, then the experience called sexual climax or sexual orgasm will be more easily attained.

Marriage manuals speak of sexual climax as something that can be ideally achieved by couples within a matter of several weeks or months of marriage. What they fail to point out is that incorrect, distorted, or unhealthy sex attitudes change very slowly and tend to prevent many women from attaining sexual climax in the first year of marriage. Some women require several years or more. If reports on frigidity in women are reliable, it would appear, moreover, that as many as one-fourth to one-third of married women never achieve climax during their entire married lives.[5] A great deal of this, however, can be

[5]W. J. Lederer and Don D. Jackson state that it is estimated by most

attributed to ignorance and misconceptions about sex and neglect of the importance of the learning process in the sex relationship.

What husbands and wives must do is love enough to learn what will meet their physical, psychological, and other needs. To focus on ideas about the sex relationship is inadequate, and to concentrate on physical processes is inadequate. Both the mind and the body must be taught through conditioning if there is going to be a satisfying sex relationship. Perhaps this is included in the biblical admonition to older married women to teach the younger women to love their husbands (Titus 2:4). *One must learn how to love.* Frequently, love does not automatically and unconsciously develop, but involves an educational process that takes time and perseverance.

Throughout the entire sex experience there must, of course, be the ingredient of self-giving love. Without it, sexual intercourse becomes meaningless and emotionally unsatisfying. Some husbands and wives have said, "Oh, yes, we both find the physical relationship satisfactory. We both achieve physical climaxes, but we are hostile toward each other in all of the other marital experiences." Sometimes it is a financial or religious problem or a case of extramarital relations that creates the dissension. Obviously, genuine love is minimal in these cases. On the other hand, there have been cases in which the physical relationships were not highly satisfactory, but where there was sufficient love so that hatred and hostility were largely absent. The loving type of relationship can best provide the psychological climate for attaining the ideal physical experience, since love usually brings patience and a willingness to learn. And in this type of atmosphere, anxiety, frustration, and inhibitions are reduced and the learning process enhanced.

physicians that more than half of all women married an average of ten years and having three children have never experienced orgasm; in *The Mirages of Marriage,* p. 124.

Sexual Satisfaction

"The one objective we have in mind for our sexual relationship," says a young husband, "is to achieve simultaneous climaxes. This is what the marriage manuals tell us is the kind of ultimate sexual experience we should seek to attain." What the young husband is saying is that a couple should be able to experience their sexual climaxes at the same moment of time, and that this should be the normal pattern for them once this is reached. This is an unfortunate misunderstanding communicated by numerous books on marriage. The basic flaw in this ideal of sex relationship is the variety of individual differences among people.

There are many factors that affect the sexual response of a woman. Among these are the demands on her emotional resources during the day, her immediate emotional relationship to her husband, the particular time of her menstrual cycle, and the distractions of thought that may occur during the sex act. Also, some women require only a few minutes to become sexually aroused; others may take up to fifteen or twenty minutes or longer. Consequently, the need for acceptance of such individual differences (including the fact that husbands and wives may reach their physical and emotional peaks at various times during sex relations) becomes all the more important. Couples should not be disappointed, however, and feel that they have failed to achieve a "compatible" sex relationship if simultaneous climaxes do not result *each time* they share in the sexual act. Husbands and wives can spare themselves many guilt feelings and unwarranted self-depreciations if this fact can be recognized and willingly accepted.

There is a great deal of learning that must take place before a husband and wife understand enough about each other's sexual responses to achieve "sexual happiness." The time needed for arousal, the proper atmosphere (some couples prefer music and lights, others do not), the words, the touches, and all the other factors that help a husband and wife reach the point of climax concurrently must be learned over a period of time because of the differences in individuals.

One psychologically based reason for rejecting pre-marital relations as a testing ground for compatibility is the fact that only after much learning has occurred about the bodily and mental processes of a person can the ideal formula be found for the achievement of a satisfying and optimum sex relationship. Intrinsic to this, also, is the requirement that love be present, along with a sense of freedom, security, and tranquillity. In practically all cases outside the marriage state there are circumstances that do not provide for a sense of freedom but are more conducive to feelings of limitation, anxiety, insecurity, and guilt. Commitment and sufficient time—sometimes months or years—are necessary before two people understand enough about each other emotionally, mentally, and physically in order to achieve the sense of sexual fulfilment they sincerely seek.

Integral to any satisfying sex relationship is what the wife feels her husband's attitude is toward the sex act. The vast majority of women hold one or two of three possible viewpoints. First, they may take the position that a husband is selfish and interested in his own sexual satisfaction. Secondly, they may hold the view that he feels guilty about the dominant position that man has held in past centuries, using a woman as a means to physical satisfaction, and, now, feeling this guilt, reluctantly cooperates with her in the sex act so that she also receives sexual gratification. A third and relatively correct view is that the climax achieved by men is of differing degrees of satisfaction; and that a man finds the greatest physical, emotional, and spiritual satisfaction when he passionately loves a woman from the depths of his being, especially when she reciprocates and returns that love from the inner depths of her being. In my experience at treating marital problems, the third view is seen in women clients on a rather infrequent basis.

Wives must somehow become aware of the need that their husbands have for loving them completely, for it fulfils some of the deepest longings of the male human spirit. As an outcome of this, there are emotional and physical experiences inexpressibly enriching and unforgettable, making an impact on the entire personality. Understanding this as she ought, a wife should lovingly accept her husband's attention and expressions of love. The husband should be aware of the dual purpose of his deep and encompassing love as it takes form in both love play and sexual intercourse. Not only does it provide him with a greater sense of personal fulfilment because it heightens the sexual experience, but it makes possible an equivalent kind of fulfilment for his wife. She needs to be wanted and loved passionately for herself as a person. When she experiences a husband's all-consuming drive to give expression to his love for her through his words, physical sensations, and emotional release, some of her deepest psychological, spiritual, and emotional needs find fulfilment and bind her increasingly closer to the one whom God has given her in marriage.

Couples interested in preparing adequately for the experience of sexual intercourse should become familiar with the data in the Masters and Johnson volume, *Human Sexual Response.* Their scientifically confirmed findings have tended to remove misconceptions and reinforce those data about sex that are generally applicable to most men and women. Three very significant outcomes of their studies involved the nature of sexual climax in the woman, the time required for her arousal, and the methods of arousal that are most effective in leading toward climax.

Contrary to many beliefs, they found that the entire area of the *mons* surrounding the clitoris was supplied with a great many sensitive nerve fibers, even as was the clitoris itself. Thus, gentle but continuous stimulation of the entire mons area with the hand was found to be an effective method of sexual arousal. Second, they found that most wives became sexually aroused if their husbands stimulated them continuously without interruption and without changing the manner or rhythm of stimulation, using as long as ten to twenty minutes or longer, if necessary. A third, correlative finding was that, despite the arguments over the advantages and disadvantages of clitoral versus vaginal climax, the greatest number of sensitive nerve endings and the most satisfying experience centered around the stimulation of the clitoris (induced by either manual love play, or, during the act of sexual intercourse, by the pubic bone of the husband striking the mons area in which the clitoris is located). Hence, prior to and during the sex act, the clitoris is of great importance to the woman in achieving climax and sexual satisfaction.

Many of the expressions of love in the form of preparation for intercourse can be found in some of the books listed in the bibliography of this volume. One must, of course, be discerning in respect to all such works, screening all suggestions through a biblically based value system. Occasionally, a husband and wife may initially reject some forms of preparatory love play only to examine them more carefully and find them acceptable. In any case, no physical or psychological coercion should be used with respect to love-making patterns. But love, time, understanding, and patience should always be present when considering these as well as other marital relationships.

Honesty and the Sex Relationship

Despite the widely held belief that husbands and wives have the ability to read each other's minds, this is seldom the attitude to take in regard to sexual matters. "He should love me so much that he should intuitively know what I want," a wife will say. Or, she will report, "It takes all the romance out of the relationship if I have to tell him I am interested in sex relations, and that I prefer this or that kind of attention." Husbands, also, hold much the same attitude. This is sheer fantasy. Mates do not possess an all-knowing ability to sense exactly what a spouse desires. As limited human beings, there are always going to be misunderstandings about the needs of others, since personality is very complex and constantly changing. Openness and honesty *must* characterize a couple's relationship if they desire the most satisfying sexual experience.

From a romantic standpoint, efforts to improve the sex relationship through self-disclosure will seem to be radically deficient. Yet one may find satisfaction in the knowledge that a husband or a wife is at least *trying* to improve the relationship. A mate, moreover, who develops a sex pattern acceptable to his spouse and continues to follow it without being reminded is, in virtually all cases, motivated by love, or he would otherwise have promptly forgotten it. The essential requirement at any stage in the marital relationship is for adequate self-disclosure, so that sexual as well as other needs can be met and personality sufficiently fulfilled.

The alternative to self-disclosure is to do as one wife who falsely claimed physical satisfaction from the sex relationship for five years because she did not wish to make her husband feel sexually inadequate. The result was frustration for her and a bitter attitude toward her husband in most of their daily relationships. Only with careful professional help were they able to open up the channels of communication so that their problem could be resolved.

In another case, a husband who denied the importance of communication and openness began a fantasy life about the nature of a sex relationship with other women. When his wife found a *Playboy* magazine in their home one day and put all the facts of their sex relationship together, she recognized the need for communication from her side. Though there was much anger and overt hostility, they were able to speak more openly and honestly, with a resulting improvement in their sex relations thereafter.

Couples should expect—and accept—the fact that sexual habits and preferences will probably change from time to time. Heredity, psychosexual development, physical health, and emotional resources are in such delicate balance that it is quite difficult for a person to predict what type of sexual pattern will be most satisfying for him at each stage of married life. Obviously, it will be even more difficult for his mate to make such predictions. Communication, which involves a determination to be open, must be employed, therefore, for a happy relationship. Variety in love play and the nature of intercourse itself become important in this regard, but only insofar as *both* mates can honestly and openly accept a particular pattern of behavior. From a Christian and a secular point of view, sexual intercourse is the right of a husband with his wife, and a wife with her husband. Beyond this, mutual agreement between husband and wife as persons in their own right should be the basis for the details of the sexual pattern which they develop.

An example of the changes which may occur involves the customary pattern of the man as the initiator of the sex relationship. It has been found that even in younger men there is a preference for their wives to approach them occasionally as an affirmation of their active interest in the sex relationship. Out of every four or five sex relationships (and sometimes even more frequently), the man prefers that his wife initiate the relationship at least once, that is, inform him through her words or her loving caresses, that she would like to engage in sexual relations. In the case of most men in their late thirties or forties, there is an increasing desire for their wives to approach them up to fifty per cent of the time for sexual intercourse. This shift in the initiating tactics from the male to the female is not only more physically arousing to the male, in most cases, but usually makes the sex relationship far more satisfying for both husband and wife. Of course, variety and the element of the unexpected tend to contribute to meeting the intimate, personal, and sexual needs of one's spouse and should not be overlooked.

Husbands and wives will find that they are often surprised at the wide variations of sexual needs that exist in their mates. The frequency of intercourse desired, the duration of the intercourse experience, the positions for intercourse, and the love play required for sexual arousal seem to differ greatly from one time to another and from one stage of life to another. As a result, husbands and wives must be continuously in communication with each other in unreserved openness—but an openness that is understanding, patient, and loving, not demanding, impatient, and hostile. If spouses wish happiness for each other, then an adequate communication pattern accompanied by a willingness on the part of each to exercise all human effort in a climate of love and self-sacrifice will usually produce remarkable results. The wife or the husband who is willing to discover the depths and the flexibility and resiliency of the human spirit through both giving and receiving love will find a greater degree of happiness than was believed possible.

The Problem of Infidelity

Occasionally, a problem of unfaithfulness develops without a spouse's knowledge. Before steps can be taken to rectify whatever may be wrong with the marriage relationship, there is a deep involvement to the point where vital and crucial decisions must be made.

What should a husband or wife do if a spouse has been unfaithful? Fight it out, separate, get a divorce? There are some guidelines that can be recommended, but the particulars of each situation are usually so unique that every person must judge the extent to which recommendations are relevant to him.

Marriage therapists, judges, and theologians appear to agree that forgiveness is the preferred response to an extramarital affair for which the individual involved is truly remorseful and has given evidence of discontinuing. Our Lord advised against breaking the marriage relationship, stating that it was because of hardness of heart that divorce was permitted, but from the beginning it was not so (Matt. 19:8).

Although it becomes increasingly difficult to maintain a marriage in the face of repeated extramarital affairs by a spouse, a mate may feel that if the affair is of a temporary nature the best decision is to reject any idea of separation or divorce. Also, if the children in the marriage are unaware of the situation, so that their moral standards are unaffected, and if the wayward spouse is close to the time when his sexual interests may be declining (usually in the forties or early fifties), he may gradually drop the affair and find relative satisfaction within his own marriage situation. Many times an honest exploration of the problem at home may adequately solve the difficulty, but if it should not, then outside and well-trained professional assistance should be sought. In general, if the mate appears to be happy with living at home, regularly desires sexual relationships, and if the news of the affair is not known by others, especially the children, the risk involved in remaining together may be much less than if divorce or separation takes place. Often, too, the third party seeks to break off the affair due to personality differences or a greater interest in another person.

For young persons in their twenties with no children, serious infidelity may warrant separation or divorce (assuming that adultery is grounds for divorce according to one's beliefs). But for spouses in their thirties or forties with children, a separation rather than a divorce creates intense hostility and a desire for the third party, who is probably willing to sympathize with the forsaken spouse. If separation, however, does occur, despite all the efforts to avoid it, loneliness and the absence of sexual inter-course usually become a problem for the woman after several months. For most men, it becomes a difficult physical problem from the very outset, and this dif-ference between the effects of the separation on men as well as on women should not be considered lightly.

If a separated couple reconciles, the husband should recognize that the willingness and desire for sexual inter-course may return very slowly to his wife. It sometimes takes several weeks or longer, and he should try to be as patient as possible during this adjustment period. Tele-vision and motion picture presentations that portray sepa-rated spouses who have been violently angry for a long period of time suddenly "making up" and forgetting the past are distortions of real life. In real life this seldom occurs. Generally, there is a *gradual* rebuilding of inter-personal relationships in which trust is reestablished, the feelings of warmth and affection slowly return, and kind-ness, patience, and understanding are mutually experi-enced.

Another misconception of reconciling couples is that of thinking that if they simply repeat some of their courtship experiences they will quickly and easily attain the same happiness which was theirs prior to marriage. "Were we not able to 'fall in love' in just a few days? We can do it again," they confidently say to themselves. What they have forgotten is that there probably were no prolonged nega-tive and hostile feelings existing prior to their courtship experiences. They started with a "clean slate," with no deep-seated problems to solve. In a reconciliation, how-ever, bitter and wounded egos must first be healed and then a start can be made in the cultivation of love and trust. Eventually, the feelings of deep love are rekindled, and, with effort and perseverance, they can once again find the happiness they enjoyed formerly.

Divorce in the case of infidelity, therefore, is to be avoided if at all possible. It should be considered only as a last resort after other resources and forms of assistance, including pastoral, medical, and psychological, have failed to provide a satisfactory solution.

A Sexual Deviation—Homosexuality

One of the most emotionally disturbing and anxiety-producing experiences—and one that is most difficult for a mate to understand—is discovering that a spouse has been involved in homosexual activity. Thoughts of divorce immediately flash through one's mind, for there is no desire to be married to a sexual deviant. After the first emotional shock wave has subsided, one should think the matter through as carefully as possible. A psychiatrist, clinical psychologist, or pastor (or a working combination of these) may be of great help at this point.

One of the first things that a husband or wife should realize is that there is a wide range of involvement for persons who engage in such activity. For example, there are many who engage in a single experience with no further incidents. There are others who may become involved a limited number of times over the whole length of their married lives. And there are still others who are confirmed homosexuals, preferring no heterosexual relationships at all. Is there a place for forgiveness? And what does the future hold regarding possible repetitions of homosexual experiences? These are the questions that one ought to ask before making any crucial decisions.

There appears to be good reason to believe that when a person is deprived of normal husband and wife relations (as is the case in prisons and such segregated situations), the chances are greater for homosexual activity to occur. But when the opportunity for normal sexual relations returns, he is capable of giving up his homosexual activities and resuming heterosexual behavior.[6] This would tend to

---

[6]James C. Coleman, *Abnormal Psychology and Modern Life,* p. 374.

give credence to the belief that isolated and infrequent homosexual experiences do not imply a hopeless situation but rather a fairly encouraging one, assuming that both spouses are interested in rebuilding their relationship.

One wife found that it was best for her to remain with her husband who had resorted on rare occasions to other men. There were several children by the marriage, and no one knew of his homosexual problem apart from herself. She and her husband had never discontinued their own normal sexual relationships, and he realized, eventually, the emotionally upsetting consequences of any revelation of his homosexual activities—breakup of marriage, loss of children, and probable loss of job. Since the risks were too great and the satisfactions derived from his marital and family life were sufficient, he pursued a normal relationship with his wife after that.

The discovery of homosexuality in a mate usually results in a complete reevaluation of the husband and wife relationship—their love play, their family backgrounds, sexual intercourse, etc. If there is sufficient determination and courage to keep the marriage intact and to improve it, a realistic discussion focused on the modification of routine or monotonous sexual experiences may well be the answer to this problem. Occasionally, a husband and wife who find their sexual interests waning in the middle years are faced with the tendency toward homosexuality in one or possibly both of them. The need for honesty and openness and great tolerance are called for in such instances, and additional help should be sought through professional channels. In the past, psychotherapy has not been highly successful in the treatment of homosexuality, but developments in the fields of psychology and psychiatry now hold out hope for treating such persons with relatively positive outcomes in many cases. In other words, if a couple is really determined to maintain their marriage and live healthy lives, there is usually a way to be found. Separation may appear to be a logical answer on one's first confrontation with this condition, but there are many other more suitable and realistic ways available for dealing with this problem. All should be tried before the tragic and damaging alternative of breaking up a marriage is chosen.

Summary

1. Human sexuality calls for men and women to fulfil their sexual roles in all areas of married life. Love of a man for a woman, and a woman for a man, takes many forms, and "sex" is a highly important form of it.
2. The physical bodies of husband and wife are means for expressing love as well as for conceiving children. Various factors may complicate or prevent the fulfilment of either of these purposes at various times in life. Generally, the *intent* at the time of marriage should be that of fulfilling both purposes.
3. Both men and women should understand that it is the nature of most males to be more sexually aggressive and in greater need of physical satisfaction than most females. Also, women should understand that husbands appreciate it if their wives are occasionally sexually aggressive toward them; and women appreciate it if husbands will at times postpone their sexual demands, depending upon circumstances.
4. Because the sexual desires and needs of husbands and wives differ, it is very important that they be willing to tell each other their needs and preferences. Husbands and wives must not expect their spouses to guess, or intuitively know, what they desire; they must tell them, particularly in the area of sex relations.
5. The frequency of sexual relations is an independent matter for each couple to work out. From clinical studies, however, it has been found that the frequency is approximately three to five times a week for those in their twenties, two to four times a week for those in their thirties, and one to three times a week in their

forties. Also, sexual intercourse can be carried on by many (but not all) couples into their sixties and seventies on a weekly or monthly basis, depending upon many factors.

6. Generally speaking, distractions from thoughts and feelings of love (pressing household duties, noise from children, poor personal hygiene, arguments, and the like) tend to interfere with satisfying sexual relations.

7. Women usually require more physical attention and love play than do men in order to be properly prepared for sexual intercourse.

8. Over the years, sexual needs and desires tend to change. Therefore, husbands and wives should constantly maintain a sense of openness and self-giving love in order to make the sexual relationship as satisfying as possible for both.

9. The problems of infidelity and sexual deviation are so complex that careful thought must be given to the choice of action to be taken or the solution to be followed. Professional help should not be overlooked in seeking solutions to such difficult marital problems. Perhaps most important is the need to evaluate thoroughly all relevant factors in the past, present, and future before any action is taken.

Selected Bibliography

Ackerman, Nathan W. *Psychodynamics of Family Life.* New York: Basic Books, 1958.

————. *Treating the Troubled Family.* New York: Basic Books, 1966.

Babbage, Stuart Barton. *Sex and Sanity.* Philadelphia: Westminster, 1965.

Bach, G. R. and P. Wyden. *The Intimate Enemy.* New York: Morrow, 1969.

Bailey, Derrick Sherwin. *The Mystery of Love and Marriage.* New York: Harper, 1952.

Barth, Karl. *The Doctrine of Creation* (*Church Dogmatics,* editors, G. W. Bromiley and T. F. Torrance, Vol. III, Part 4). Edinburgh: T. & T. Clark, 1961.

Berelson, B. and G. A. Steiner. *Human Behavior.* New York: Harcourt, Brace & World, 1964.

Berkhof, L. *Systematic Theology.* Grand Rapids: Eerdmans, 1953.

Berne, Eric. *Games People Play.* New York: Grove, 1964.

Bloom, B. S. *Stability and Change in Human Characteristics.* New York: John Wiley, 1964.

Bovet, T. *A Handbook to Marriage.* Garden City, New York: Dolphin Books, 1958.

Brecher, Ruth and Edward (editors). *An Analysis of Human Sexual Response.* New York: Signet, 1966.

Brunner, Emil. *The Divine Imperative.* Philadelphia: Westminster, 1947.

————. *Faith, Hope, and Love.* Philadelphia: Westminster, 1956.

Buhler, Charlotte. *Values in Psychotherapy.* New York: The Free Press of Glencoe, 1962.

Colby, Kenneth M. *A Primer for Psychotherapists.* New York: Ronald, 1951.

Coleman, James C. *Abnormal Psychology and Modern Life.* New York: Scott-Foresman, 1956.

Davitz, J. R. *The Communication of Emotional Meaning.* New York: McGraw-Hill, 1964.

Dicks, Henry V. *Marital Tensions.* New York: Basic Books, 1967.

Dominian, J. *Marital Breakdown.* Baltimore: Penguin, 1968.

Erikson, Erik H. *Childhood and Society.* New York: Norton, 1950.

————. *Identity and the Life Cycle (Psychological Issues,* Vol. I, No. 1). New York: International Universities Press, 1959.

————. *Insight and Responsibility.* New York: Norton, 1964.

Feucht, O. E. (editor). *Sex and the Church.* St. Louis: Concordia, 1961.

Foote, Nelson N. and Leonard S. Cottrell. *Identity and Interpersonal Competence.* Chicago: U. of Chicago Press, 1955.

Frankl, Viktor E. *The Doctor and the Soul.* New York: Knopf, 1965.

Greene, Bernard L. (editor). *The Psychotherapies of Marital Disharmony.* New York: Free Press, 1965.

Gulick, L. H. and L. Urwick (editors). *Papers on the Science of Administration.* New York: Institute of Public Administration, Columbia University, 1937.

Haley, J. *Strategies of Psychotherapy.* New York: Grune & Stratton, 1964.

Hansen, P. G., *et al. Engagement and Marriage.* St. Louis: Concordia, 1959.

Hiltner, S. and K. Menninger (editors). *Constructive Aspects of Anxiety.* Nashville: Abingdon, 1963.

Homans, Peter (editor). *The Dialogue Between Theology and Psychology.* Chicago: U. of Chicago Press, 1968.

Howe, Reuel L. *The Creative Years.* New York: Seabury, 1965.

————. *Herein is Love.* Valley Forge: Judson, 1961.

————. *The Miracle of Dialogue.* New York: Seabury, 1963.

Jourard, Sidney M. *Personal Adjustment.* New York: Macmillan, 1963.

————. *The Transparent Self.* Princeton: Van Nostrand, 1964.

Kessel, N. and H. Walton. *Alcoholism.* Baltimore: Penguin Books, 1965.

Kinsey, A., *et al. Sexual Behavior in the Human Female.* Philadelphia: Saunders, 1953.

Lederer, William J. and Don D. Jackson. *The Mirages of Marriage.* New York: Norton, 1968.

London, Perry and Robert K. Bower, "Altruism, Extraversion and Mental Illness." *The Journal of Social Psychology,* LXXVI (October 1968), 19-30.

London, Perry. *The Modes and Morals of Psychotherapy.* New York: Holt, Rinehart and Winston, 1964.

Mace, David R. *Whom God Hath Joined.* Philadelphia: Westminster, 1953.

Maslow, A. H. *Motivation and Personality.* New York: Harper, 1954.

————. *Religions, Values, and Peak-Experiences.* Columbus: Ohio State U. P., 1964.

Masters, William H. and Virginia E. Johnson. *Human Sexual Response.* Boston: Little-Brown, 1966.

Miller, Keith. *The Taste of New Wine.* Waco: Word, 1965.

Mowrer, O. Hobart. *The New Group Therapy.* Princeton: Van Nostrand, 1964.

Mudd, E. H. and A. Krich (editors). *Man and Wife.* New York: Norton, 1957.

Nash, E. M., *et al. Marriage Counseling in Medical Practice.* Chapel Hill: U. of North Carolina Press, 1964.

Peterson, James A. *Married Love in the Middle Years.* New York: Association, 1968.

Piper, Otto A. *The Biblical View of Sex and Marriage.* New York: Scribners, 1960.

Rogers, Carl R. *Client-Centered Therapy.* Boston: Houghton-Mifflin, 1951.

————. *On Becoming a Person.* Boston: Houghton-Mifflin, 1961.

Ruesch, J. *Therapeutic Communication.* New York: Norton, 1961.

Satir, V. *Conjoint Family Therapy.* Palo Alto: Science and Behavior Books, 1964.

Selye, Hans. *Stress of Life.* New York: McGraw-Hill, 1956.

Sherrill, Lewis J. *Guilt and Redemption.* Richmond: John Knox, 1957.

Shostrom, Everett L. *Man, the Manipulator.* Nashville: Abingdon, 1967.

Stone, Hannah M. and Abraham. *A Marriage Manual.* New York: Simon and Schuster, 1953.

Thielicke, Helmut. *The Ethics of Sex.* Translated by John W. Doberstein. New York: Harper, 1964.

Tournier, Paul. *A Doctor's Casebook in the Light of the Bible.* Translated by Edwin Hudson. New York: Harper, 1954.

————. *Secrets.* Richmond: John Knox, 1964.

————. *To Understand Each Other.* Translated by John S. Gilmour. Richmond: John Knox, 1967.

Van De Velde, Th. H. *Ideal Marriage: Its Physiology and Technique.* Translated by Stella Browne. New York: Random House, 1957.

White, Ernest. *Christian Life and the Unconscious.* New York: Harper, 1955.